INSPIRED *by*
The PASSION *Test*

INSPIRED

by

The
PASSION
Test

The #1 Tool for
Discovering Your
Passion and Purpose

Janet Bray Attwood, Geoff Affleck, Ulrike Berzau,
Patty Blakesley, Elayna Fernández, Shivani Gupta,
Carol Haave, Ratika Hansen, Jill Hughes,
Susanne Knudsen, Snježana Kurešević, Yves Nager,
Deborah (Dee) Redding, Veronique Scheldeman,
Karen Smith & Jens-Simon Ulvoy.

(P)

INSPIRED *by The* PASSION *Test*
The #1 Tool for Discovering Your Passion and Purpose

Published by Persona Publishing.

ISBN 978-0-99858-231-3 paperback
ISBN 978-0-99858-232-0 eBook

Compiled by:
Geoff Affleck
www.geoffaffleck.com

Edited by:
Page Two
www.pagetwostrategies.com

Cover Design by:
Rachel Lopez
www.r2cdesign.com

Interior Design by:
Bonnie Bushman
The Whole Caboodle Graphic Design

We dedicate this book to our families and friends who have supported our journeys. Knowing that there are no mistakes in the Universe, it is our joy to offer these stories, advice and tools to those who have been drawn to these pages and who are ready to choose in favor of their passions.

Learn more about The Passion Test at
www.thepassiontest.com

TABLE OF CONTENTS

Chapter 1

THE BIRTH OF PASSION
Janet Bray Attwood

"What you love and God's will for you are one and the same."
—The Passion Test

*R*ealizing what this statement really means is the fundamental secret to discovering your life's purpose. Your passions, the things you love and care about most, are the bread crumbs that lead you on to living that purpose.

All of us have been raised with so many false concepts about what it takes to be happy that sometimes it's a real challenge to let go and follow our hearts.

1

Many years ago I was working in a job I hated. My office was filled with recruiters making tens of thousands of dollars every month. Each time a placement was made for another disk drive engineer, the bell would ring. But it never rang for me.

One day I saw a poster for a success seminar. Something about it struck a chord. The next day I called in sick to work and drove an hour and a half to the event.

Sitting up front I listened as a beautiful, articulate woman spoke about how easy it can be to enjoy success. The speaker said you just have to find those things that light you up inside—your passions.

She then described a study of 100 very successful people. The study found the one thing all those successful people had in common was that they all were living the five things they considered to be most important.

Immediately, a lightbulb went off in my head. *If I can just get clear about the five things that are most important to me, that will be the first step for my own success!* I thought.

And in that moment The Passion Test was born.

Little did I dream then that this thought would ultimately become a *New York Times* bestselling book with more than 2,000 facilitators in more than 63 countries.

But what filled my mind at that moment was: *This is it! This is my passion, my purpose in life—to be a speaker, like this amazing woman.*

I'll find a way to get her to hire me, I thought, *Even if I have to follow her all over the country and attend every one of her seminars.*

At the end of the seminar when she asked if anyone could give her a ride to the airport, my hand shot up. *This is my chance to get her to be my mentor*, I thought.

But, on the drive to the airport, there wasn't any natural opportunity to ask her. Finally, when we got to the airport, she said, "Janet, what's your dream?" I immediately replied, "Well, you better hire me because otherwise I'm going to become your biggest competition."

Right at that moment, an announcement came over the speakers that her plane was boarding. Without saying anything more, she gave me a hug and went to board her plane.

I was left the airport feeling like I had just put a big foot in my mouth. Driving home all I could think about was how I had just blown my chance to follow my dreams.

But, by the next morning, I'd decided nothing was going to stop me, so when a friend casually asked how I was doing, I answered with excitement, "I've found my calling! I'm going to be a speaker."

I told my friend about my plan to follow this speaker around the country until she had no choice but to hire me. The only challenge was that I had no money. "But I know I'll manage it somehow. I just know it," I told my friend.

The next day, I was sitting with my eyes closed in meditation at the local TM center when I felt small pieces of paper falling on my head. I opened my eyes to discover my friend showering me with ten $100 bills, laughing and saying, "Merry Christmas, go live your dream."

I did travel across the country and was finally hired by the woman I so admired. Today, that woman, Debra Poneman, is one of my best friends, and I am living my dream of being a speaker and transformational leader.

But it's been a winding road, and along the way I've learned there is one key secret to living a happy, fulfilling, rewarding life: "Whenever you're faced with a choice, a decision or an opportunity, choose in favor of your passions."

There are two parts to this. First, you have to know what you're passionate about, what it is that matters most to you in your life. That's why my business partner, Chris Attwood, and I wrote *The Passion Test: The Effortless Path to Discovering Your Destiny.* The Passion Test is a simple, yet powerful way to clarify your top passions in life.

The second part is to choose in favor of those passions. When you do this consistently with every significant decision, you will be guaranteed a passionate life.

My friends Stewart Emery, Mark Thompson, and Jerry Porras wrote a fabulous book called *Success Built to Last: Creating a Life That Matters.* They interviewed over 300 people who have enjoyed enduring success for more than twenty years. People like former Presidents Jimmy Carter and Bill Clinton, Senator John McCain, Michael Dell, Bill Gates, Lance Armstrong, and many others.

All of these very successful people had one important characteristic in common: when faced with a major decision in their life, they always made their choice based on what held deep meaning for them. This is what we mean by choosing in favor of your passions.

Sometimes, when you listen to all the advice that's available about what is necessary to create a happy, fulfilling, successful life, it can be a bit overwhelming. When you boil it down, if you're able to do nothing else, clarify your passions and then choose in favor of them, and you will discover your life unfolding in exciting, new, unexpected ways.

I can't guarantee you'll have hundred-dollar bills showered on your head, but I can guarantee that your life will be more rewarding than you can ever imagine.

Does that mean there won't be challenges? Deciding to choose in favor of your passions is just the beginning . . .

How Passion Leads You

After I followed Debra all over the country, she finally said, "You're hired!" and I knew my life was going to change forever. The question was, "How?"

I went back home, packed up all my things, put them in my little Toyota, and started driving to Los Angeles where Debra was based. I hadn't gone 20 miles when my car just stopped.

Turns out it had thrown a rod, was beyond repair, and I was left without a vehicle. I had just enough money to buy a train ticket to L.A. so that's what I did.

I arrived at Debra's door as she was packing to take off on one of her many trips. Telling me to make myself at home and giving me the keys to her car, she left. I had been too embarrassed to tell her I now only had $13 to my name.

Not knowing what to do and having always loved the beautiful grounds at Yogananda's center in Pacific Palisades, I went there to see if some inspiration would strike. Along the paths in the gardens there were little donation boxes. As I sat on a bench next to one, I thought, *Well, $13 is not going to get me very far. I might as well just give it all up to God.*

So I dropped my last $13 in the donation box with a little prayer asking God to take care of me and that somehow everything would be okay.

I drove home, now literally penniless, and feeling like such a dope. *What have I done?*

When I got home I rationed out my food because I didn't know how long it would be until I was able to get some more money. Then my phone rang.

"Hi, Janet, I've driven up from San Diego. I'm here in Santa Monica and I'd love to take you to lunch," the voice said. Finally figuring out that the voice belonged to Francis, my ex-husband's father, I said, "Oh Francis, thanks so much, but now's not a very good time."

"Oh come on, Janet. It'll be fun and you have to eat anyway," Francis told me.

Thinking he was right, I DID have to eat somehow and what could it hurt, I said, "Okay, but you have to come pick me up."

Francis arrived a little while later and we went to lunch. Through lunch all he could talk about was this exciting new business he was in, and that the products he was selling were amazing, herbal weight-loss products that really worked. A company called Herbalife, a network marketing company that was just getting started at the time, made the products.

"Francis, I so appreciate you thinking of me, but it's just not possible right now because I don't have any money to buy the products," I told him.

"That doesn't matter. I'll front you $500 worth of product to get you started. I just know you will do great at this, Janet," was his reply.

At that moment, our waitress came to the table to see if there was anything we needed. She was a pleasant and significantly overweight young woman. Seeing all the Herbalife bottles that Francis had on the table, she said, "What's that?"

I proceeded to tell her all the things Francis had just told me.

She listened, obviously intrigued. When I was done, she said, "I'll take it."

And right there I sold $100 worth of products and I was back on my way to solvency once again.

I tell this story because it helps illustrate that following your passions is not always a perfectly straight road. My passion was to become a transformational speaker, helping people change their lives for the better all over the world.

I had quit my job, moved all my belongings, and taken some big risks to follow my passion. And I ended up with nothing.

However, I got to a place where it was so clear that I didn't know what to do next and that allowed me to completely surrender, which is what giving away my last $13 was for me.

When I gave up and let go, then this powerful force of evolution that is guiding and directing all of our lives took over.

Out of the blue, I was provided with the means that allowed me to go on and begin a career that has brought me so much fulfillment.

So, as you're feeling down and dejected, remember, "What you love and God's will for you are one and the same."

Follow your heart, let go, and be open to what shows up.

Janet Bray Attwood is a visionary, a transformational leader, and a world humanitarian. She is co-author of the New York Times bestsellers, The Passion Test: The Effortless Path to Discovering Your Life Purpose *and* Your Hidden Riches: Unleashing the Power of Ritual to Create a Life of Meaning and Purpose. *Janet has trained almost 2,000 certified Passion Test facilitators in more than 60 countries.*

Janet has spoken on how to discover passion and purpose throughout the world and has shared the stage with His Holiness the 14th Dalai Lama, Dr. Stephen Covey, Richard Branson, Nobel Peace Prize winner F.W. de Klerk, Jack Canfield, Zappo's CEO Tony Hsieh, Rev. Michael Beckwith, and many others. She is also a founding member of the Transformational Leadership Council.

For her ongoing work with homeless women and youth in lockdown detention centers, Janet received the highest award for volunteer service in the U.S., The President's Volunteer Service Award *from the President of the United States.*

Janet is a living example of what it means to live with an open heart and mind. Learn more at www.thepassiontest.com.

Chapter 2

WHAT TO DO WHEN YOUR LIFE FEELS LIKE A GAME OF WHACK-A-MOLE

Carol A. Haave

My life had become a game of whack-a-mole, and I was the mole. It started when my dad died in 2009. I felt this energy slam through my body and knew the man I adored was gone. Six months later, my husband's son (my stepson), Doug, died of sepsis from a superbug, *Streptococcus pneumoniae*. His wife, who is from Iraq, was seven months pregnant and had no family in the U.S. She moved in with us, with their four-year-old daughter. Not long after, my mother died, my husband's mother died, my marriage crumbled, and a valued long-term business partnership blew up. It seemed like every time I popped my head up—whack! Smacked back down again.

There were days I didn't want to get out of bed. If I didn't have to go to the grocery store or walk my very precocious Portuguese water dog, Lexi, I wouldn't have left the house. I was struggling to get my feet under me, to focus on something good, to maybe even do something different—something that made me happy. When I wasn't sleeping (which was a lot), I researched online. How to deal with overwhelming grief. How to save your marriage (approximately 90 percent of couples who lose a child divorce). How to discover your purpose in life. It was then that I stumbled across the Passion Test. It was April 2011. "Discover your top five passions and create a life of meaning and joy." I was in!

At that time, I was no longer working for the government and was looking to do something different, something new, anything but the life I'd been living for the past couple of years. I've always known that I had a destiny, that I was here on the planet for a reason, and my life's purpose couldn't possibly be complete. I had accomplished so much, learned how to be successful in a man's world, reached professional heights I never thought possible. Sure, I had been dealt some blows (my psychologist was amazed I was still standing), but I was strong, independent, and determined to find my way—plus, I had all these credentials and work experience.

I had always experimented with how to make my organizations perform better, trying different ideas and methodologies. The Passion Test would simply be another tool of many in the box. What I didn't realize was how beautifully simple and elegant the process is. When Janet and Chris say you will learn tools that you can use for the rest of your life, it's absolutely true.

I didn't read the book, though I bought it. I didn't take the online test, even though I went to the website. I did talk with a certified Passion Test facilitator, because I wanted more information about the certification course. And then I took the first step toward my recovery—something just for me. I signed up for a three-day weekend in Chicago to become a certified Passion Test facilitator. Learn to know; teach to grow. I needed to do both!

I believe that each of us has innate skills, talents, gifts, and abilities. Our job is to figure out what they are and use them to benefit ourselves, our family, our community, and the world. So the Passion Test seemed right up my alley. Besides, they said I couldn't fail the test, and God knows it seemed like I had been failing a lot lately.

The very first time I did the Passion Test was during that certification weekend. I felt like I was wrapped up in a warm blanket in winter. I'd been to many workshops, but this one was different. Facilitators Janet, Beth, and Cheryl created a safe, loving, fun, and intimate space for people to learn, share, and practice being in front of a room. The weekend was filled with positivity, camaraderie, laughter, and play—just what I needed to begin healing.

I was looking for something to ground me, something I could hold on to that would help me remember why I was here. At that time, I wrote, *When my life is ideal, I am*

1. *Fully engaged in what I'm doing,*
2. *Supporting others in their work,*

3. *Making a meaningful contribution,*
4. *Using my best skills and talents, and*
5. *Working with people I like and trust in a supportive environment.*

My plan became to create my own training programs for women who want to be change agents in their organizations, using the Passion Test as the foundational tool. Surely, if there were more competent, passionate, compassionate, and courageous women in charge, the world would be a wildly different place. I started holding workshops and could see they were making a noticeable and significant difference in the lives of those who attended. For example, one woman's passion was to live in Colorado—she moved lock, stock, and barrel three weeks later. I began taking courses on marketing, online content creation, and selling from the stage. I met new friends, and my life was slowly turning around, until...

In 2012, my husband, Terry, and I had just started marriage counseling (what we really needed was grief counseling) when he contracted a never-seen-before strain of *E. coli* that went septic. Of course, my stepdaughter, Meredith, and I didn't know this for more than a week after he went on life support with a less than 10 percent chance to live.

Now I found myself in the critical care ward with a soon-to-be ex-husband who was probably going to die from a blood infection like his son. His liver stopped functioning because that's where the *E. coli* began its assault on his body. A machine was breathing for him because his lungs no longer worked. He was on dialysis as his kidneys failed. And the doctors were giving him a drug of last resort to keep his heart pumping! There were tubes and drains and wires and beeps and squeaks and odd-colored fluids. As a woman who never had children of her own because she couldn't figure out how to get past the stinky diapers, spit up, and vomit without throwing up herself, I was definitely in uncharted territory.

I had been a deputy undersecretary of defense for Counterintelligence and Security, as well as the assistant secretary for International Affairs at Homeland Security. I had spent my career traveling the world, transitioning advanced technology during times of conflict. I was strong, athletic, smart, and the consummate problem solver and change agent. So what did I do? I relied on my training and went into mission mode, just as I did when anything else fell apart.

It's recommended that you do the Passion Test every six months, but I didn't have to—it was clear that my passion in that moment was to save my husband's life. I loved him and couldn't imagine my life without him.

The Passion Test teaches a concept: Intention, Attention, No Tension. My *intention* was to save his life *and* as much of his limbs as possible. The "leave them for dead" drug of last resort used to bolster his heart had resulted in gangrene in his hands and feet because it diverted blood from his extremities to his core organs. My *attention* was focused on finding him the best care and protocols available. And, frankly, the *no tension* part sneaked into the process simply because I was so exhausted.

Terry is a retired Navy SEAL who didn't smoke or drink and was in good shape. I knew he would do his part to get better because he's stubborn that way, and we—Meredith and I, and the healthcare providers—needed to do ours. In truth, my original passions still applied:

Did I have to be fully engaged in what I was doing? You bet.

Was I supporting others in their work? Yes. I sometimes knew more about what was going on with my husband than the nurses or doctors who only saw him periodically, and I was proposing alternative protocols suggested by outside experts, such as the use of a hyperbaric chamber to oxygenize his limbs (they loved that—not!—though those alternatives played a huge role in the final outcome).

Was trying to save his life a meaningful contribution? He would say yes and does every day, always telling people that I'm his guardian angel.

Did it require the best use of my skills and talents? Absolutely. I was on a steep learning curve, quizzing nurse and doctor friends, reading medical research papers, praying—all in pursuit of the best care I could get for him.

Was I working with people I liked and trusted in a supportive environment? This wasn't exactly the team concept I had in mind, but, for the most part, the answer was yes.

Eckhart Tolle talks about the "power of now" and being fully present in each moment. This was it. I couldn't read a magazine or book. I couldn't watch TV. Meredith and I took to Facebook to update friends and family on Terry's condition because there wasn't enough time in the day to respond to all the requests for information. We slept on recliner chairs in critical care for almost a month, waiting for his "numbers" to improve, for him to wake up. I convinced the pulmonary doctor to see whether he could breathe on his own. He'd had a tube down his throat for a couple of weeks, and the doctors were pushing to do a tracheotomy, which meant slicing open his neck and which comes with its own set of problems. In my heart, I knew that he could do it, that he could wake up and breathe on his own. The day he did was joyous.

He wasn't out of the woods yet, though. The following year he had severe pancreatitis with complications and didn't eat or drink for six months—when he wasn't in the hospital, I was feeding him intravenously at home. I devoted my attention to learning everything about sepsis, pancreatitis, and the complications resulting from both. I knew when he was becoming septic—and saved his life on more than one occasion when doctors didn't detect the problem. I fired doctors who were incompetent and nurses who didn't wash their hands. In total, this ordeal lasted three years. Nurses even suggested I take the nursing exam—they thought I could pass. It was, to say the least, a learning experience!

So here's what I learned:

1. You're stronger, smarter, braver, and more capable than you think. You will figure it out one step at a time. You will do what you do best.
2. Intention, Attention, No Tension is essential, and it can happen naturally when you're in crisis mode.
3. You'll know something when there is a reason for you to know it. My grandmother was a Christian Scientist, and my mother was a pragmatist, so I didn't have a lot of experience with doctors growing up. Terry's condition was way out of my knowledge zone, but I trusted and had faith that my prayers would be answered and miracles would occur.
4. Your body will let you know the direction that's right for you at the time. I could sense when information

I received wasn't right—my body would tense up. The Passion Test calls this Nature's Guidance System. Expansion and contraction are simple ways to get in touch with that still, small voice within that has the answers you're looking for.

5. You must find your voice and be unafraid to speak. If I had not taken charge and demanded action when I knew he was septic, my husband would have died. I now teach how to speak out in my Lead from Any Position course.

6. Every patient in a hospital needs an advocate. Patients are too sick to do it for themselves. There was a doctor who yelled at my husband for not eating during his severe pancreatitis. She removed his IV for several hours, which ultimately necessitated an additional surgery to upsize the pancreatic drain because the fluids inside the cyst had congealed. You must, must, must be that advocate for your loved one. That doctor was fired and replaced by the medical director of the hospital.

7. Ask for help and support, but don't be overwhelmed by it. Rely on your friends who are doctors, nurses, alternative practitioners, spiritual counselors, and anyone else you think can help you with the situation. You will also need help with the household that you're not able to take care of. For example, a veterinary technician at Lexi's doggie day care took her home for extended periods while I was at the hospital—Caitlin is

still a godsend. The beauty of unselfish acts and seeming coincidences is that they are miracles sent to you at just the right time.

8. Take care of and be gentle with yourself. There is a reason the airlines tell you to put your oxygen mask on first. I was blessed to have a nurse friend take the night shift with my husband, even though I was in the room. Diane knew I needed both medical help and sleep—she was also a godsend! She came without my asking, paid for her plane ticket, never asked for reimbursement, and stayed as long as we needed. I can never repay her and hope that you are fortunate enough to have friends like that.

9. Getting clear on your passions will guide your life in a direction that has deep meaning for you. Just be prepared to stay open, because it may not look the way you think it will.

My passions haven't changed much since then; maybe how I've worded them and how they've manifested in my life has. Today, when my life is ideal, I am

1. Happy, happy, happy;
2. Making a difference in the lives of people every day;
3. In love and loved unconditionally and supportively;
4. Thin, trim, tanned, and toned; and
5. Taking advantage of opportunities that speak to my soul.

I am all those things... except maybe for the thin, trim, tanned, and toned part. I'm still working on that. And my husband and I are together and stronger than ever.

Carol A. Haave is a certified Passion Test facilitator for adults, businesses, kids, and teens. Formerly the deputy undersecretary of defense for Counterintelligence and Security, and the assistant secretary for International Affairs at the Department of Homeland Security, Carol now teaches aspiring women how to be leaders and change agents in their organizations—and reap the rewards. She has a master's degree in human resources management and a bachelor's degree in sociology. You can learn more about her at www.sagesforchange.com.

Chapter 3

THE PASSION TO LIVE

Snježana Kurešević

"There is no passion to be found playing small—in settling for a life that is less than the one you are capable of living."
—Nelson Mandela

It was the first time I was going to meet Janet Attwood. Every cell of my body tingled with joy, excitement, and anticipation while I was getting ready for that long-awaited encounter. After all, I was about to be mentored by one of the world's famous leaders in transformation! What was she going to be like in person? What was she going to tell me? What was she going to wear?

19

While I was waiting for my video call with Janet, I closed my eyes for a moment. My mind wandered back to when I was an eleven-year-old girl. At that time, a dreadful civil war in my home country, Bosnia-Herzegovina, hit the breaking news headlines all over the world. Little did I know that such a horrifying event would lead me to endless adventures, to discovering the world, and even to meeting Janet Attwood.

The war started unexpectedly. One day, my class at school was interrupted by a shrill alarm. I felt my head spinning, and terrible sensations of fear, panic, and confusion penetrated my body. A series of explosions broke out, and pieces of glass rained down on the screaming children.

As I walked home under the rainfall of bombs, the homes around me looked like collapsing houses of cards. People on the street seemed helpless in their attempts to protect their ears and their bodies.

In the following months, I learned to survive with limited food and water, and without electricity. I learned to recognize the sound of a bomb when it was dangerously close, and to throw myself on the ground and wait for it to explode. I learned to invent social games during long nights in the bomb shelter. But most important, I learned how precious life is. I watched people living every moment on edge, not knowing if there would be a tomorrow. Their dreams of having a big house and an expensive car were replaced by dreams of being free and alive. The only thing they were left with was the present moment.

It was in those days of war that I discovered my passion to live. To paint my life with the colors of love, adventure, and joy. I decided to honor life and, one day, when the war was over, to live and play big. To not wait for tomorrow. After all, that tomorrow may never come.

And so I did. I always diligently followed my plan to live life fully. I used every opportunity to travel, and when there was none, I somehow created one.

I went on to work for a big international company; I have lived in different countries and made wonderful friendships all over the world. Yet, with time, I would wake up and wonder if that was all there was to life. Wonder if I was truly happy. Wonder if in the years to come I should settle down and start living the dream of the Western world: have a family, a beautiful house, a fancy car, and a sexy business card.

Not that I didn't want those things. Oh yes, I wanted every single one of them. But something was missing in that picture, something that would get me out of bed without me pressing the snooze button six times. I figured that wondering whether I was happy probably meant I wasn't. Maybe it was only a temporary feeling of emptiness because my country had once again grabbed public attention, this time with a disastrous flood, and the story of war started haunting me again. Was my country ever going to have peace? I felt guilty for living abroad and not being there to share the suffering with my family.

One lazy Sunday afternoon, while I was looking for a good book to read in the park, I stumbled upon *Happy for No Reason* by Marci Shimoff. Marci shared a touching story about a woman from Iraq who had been a victim of violence and who turned her pain into the most noble and graceful act I could ever imagine. Instead of going on their honeymoon, the Iraqi woman and her husband decided to use their savings to help women affected by the war in my country. Soon they founded a large international organization to help women victims of war all around the world. Tears rolled down my cheeks as old memories surfaced. I noticed a strange feeling in my body, a feeling of despair mixed with incredible excitement. What if I went through that horrible war so that I could help somebody else? What if I could also share my story and inspire people all around the world to live their dreams? What if I could even write a book?

My memories were interrupted by an incoming video call. Janet's picture appeared on the screen. Beautiful long red hair; perfectly matching lipstick; eyes filled with life, wisdom, and most of all, playfulness. I pinched myself to make sure I wasn't dreaming.

"So, you want to write a book?" Janet asked.

"Well, yes," I replied. "It's only that I don't know anything about writing and publishing books. Let's discuss something more realistic, something I actually have a chance of achieving."

Janet seemed to ignore my comment, instructed me to complete a short exercise, and asked me to reconnect in five minutes.

A feeling of fear and disillusionment took over my mind. Was I being childish to expect so much out of this meeting? What was I thinking? There she was, a *New York Times* bestselling author who shared the stage with the world-famous success and leadership experts, even with the Dalai Lama. Of course in her world it was possible to accomplish anything. She probably could not even imagine what it felt like to be just another somebody, to be me. Even if she could have imagined it, she must have forgotten that feeling a long time ago.

Another thought crossed my mind. How was I going to inspire and support others to live their dreams if I thought my own dream was beyond my reach? But maybe it really was unrealistic to think I could reach for the stars, at least right away. Maybe I needed to start small and see what would happen. I wanted to write a book, but I had never written one before. I wanted to be a transformational leader just like Janet, but then, how many people have that dream and how many actually achieve it?

The five-minute break was up. I looked at my computer screen, and I froze, with my mouth wide open. I could not believe my eyes. Another beautiful woman was sitting next to Janet. That woman was none other than Marci Shimoff!

This can't be, I thought to myself.

Marci was visiting Janet in Denmark, and I found myself in the midst of a wonderful conversation with these two ladies.

That day, Janet taught me a principle that would change my life forever: when you feel truly passionate about something, you will always have the ability to create it in your life. And she did it in her own unique way, with little words and by lighting up my heart with such a sweet miracle.

In the following year, I had the privilege of spending a lot of time with Janet, either at retreats and conferences around the world or at her house in Denmark. None of these encounters was like the others. Her humor and infinite love made each occasion unique and special. I felt that she was in flow, and being with her, so was I.

One day, I was about to head to the Passion Test facilitator workshops in Denmark and Finland, where I had the privilege of presenting as part of my training with Janet. On my way to the airport, I stopped at the front door of my apartment and looked at the colorful map of my top five passions in life, which I had discovered during my mentorship with Janet:

1. Living a legendary romance with my fabulous soul partner
2. Having fun with everything I do
3. Being surrounded by inspiring, passionate, and successful people
4. Working closely with the top transformational leaders in the world
5. Traveling the world first-class

A feeling of infinite gratitude filled my body. It had not even been a year since I had discovered the Passion Test, yet in that very moment, I was living ALL my passions full-out.

My eyes glanced over one of the markers that I had previously identified as evidence that I was living my passions fully: "I am picking an outfit for events at which I am presenting together with the top transformational leaders in the world." I had just picked the outfits for the workshops at which I was about to present with Janet Attwood! I was about to travel to two different countries, where I would meet the most inspiring, passionate, and successful people I could ever dream of, from established coaches and trainers to successful authors and entrepreneurs. Needless to say, having lots of fun was guaranteed. And guess what? My fabulous partner, whom I had met a few months prior, gave me a ride to the airport. What about my dream to share my message with others? The book you are holding in your hands made that dream come true.

Sitting on the plane, I reflected: What was it that led to these moments of success, to that feeling that my life is on purpose? Let me share with you what I discovered.

Own Your Story

All my life, I have wondered why that terrible war had to happen to me. What I learned was to embrace my story just as it is, instead of using that story as an excuse to stop me from creating what I want for myself. I now know that everything that happened in my life has led me to where I am today. Not only that, but being in a war zone was actually a precious gift. During the war, I learned to appreciate life in its entire beauty. I witnessed the dreams of people around me fall apart, and it was then that the burning desire in my heart was born to help others step up to their full potential. During the time I spent in Germany as a refugee, I discovered my passion for exploring new cultures, and this passion has led me to the most amazing places on this planet.

The moment when I looked at my past from this angle, all the pain suddenly disappeared and new opportunities opened up. There was no more resistance within me, nothing more to fight, and it seemed as though the pain had lost any interest in paying me further visits.

Maybe you have a similar story. Maybe your parents went through a painful divorce while you were a child. Or you went to medical school, but all you ever really wanted was to play piano. Maybe you have to fight a difficult illness, or you can't seem to find your perfect partner and you wander from one painful relationship to the next. How has your story served you so far? What gifts have you received? How are you unique because of it?

What Would You *Really* Love?

If you are like most people, you are not always sure what you really want to create for yourself. Or maybe you're pretty sure that you're going for everything you want, yet for some reason, you don't feel excited. The reason may be that secretly you would love something else, but that something seems to be just out of your reach.

When you feel empty or not excited, it's your passions calling for your attention. You can try to convince them that right now is not a good time, that once you take care of more important things you'll come back to them. Or you can decide to listen to your passions carefully. Sometimes they'll tell you that it's time for you to embark on a new journey and pursue a new direction. Sometimes they'll want you to stay on course and dream bigger. Sometimes they'll lead you to spending more time with your loved ones. And sometimes they'll simply tell you to go to bed.

A simple way that you can start paying more attention to your passions is to speak to yourself from your heart. Next time you ask yourself, *What should I do?* imagine that your heart, and not your mind, is asking this question. Here are some examples:

Mind-centered question:	Heart-centered question:
What should I do?	What would I love to do?
How can I take care of my family?	How can I take care of my family and myself?
How can I gain more confidence?	How can I love myself more?
What should my next career step be?	Who would I like to be?
Should I take that new job offer?	Will that job bring me closer to my passions?
How can I find more time?	What are the situations I would love to say no to more often?
How can I make others appreciate me?	How can I show up as who I truly am and who I want to be?

Listening to your passions may be frightening because sometimes they'll ask you to face the unknown. Sometimes they'll come up with a vision that seems much greater than yourself. What I've learned is that just because something you really love seems out of reach for the moment, it doesn't mean you should compromise, downplay your passion, or pretend it doesn't exist. It's what you love and the way you express it that make you unique. When you have the courage to be unique, to own your story, and to own what you love, life becomes a game with endless possibilities. Will you lean in and pay attention to your passions, or will you settle for a life that is less than the one you are capable of living?

Here's to your passion to live!

Snježana Kurešević is a leadership development expert and training facilitator. She has worked as a global project manager for a number of human capital development programs in large international organizations. Snježana is passionate about inspiring and empowering individuals and organizations to maximize their potential by following their purpose. She is a certified Passion Test facilitator and a Master Trainer for the Passion Test Certification Course, and has graduated with a degree in economics. Born in Bosnia Herzegovina, she now lives in Germany and enjoys fitness, traveling and connecting with personal development and leadership authorities around the world. Connect with Snježana at snjezana.kuresevic@ gmail.com.

BREAKING DOWN THE WALLS:
HOW I FOUND TRUE LOVE

Karen Smith

*"With the drawing of this Love and the voice of this Calling
We shall not cease from exploration"*
—T.S. Eliot

J've always explored the magic of life with curiosity. I left home at sixteen and made money by painting T-shirts to sell to my schoolmates. About a year later, I got a television gig doing live demonstrations to recruit students for the textile design school I was starting. At this time, I didn't have much fear; I was just following my heart. I learned then that anything was possible.

Years later, I opened a store to sell my hand-designed clothing line. The store became so popular, I wound up buying and selling clothing, and then I opened a second store.

I was a true natural-born creative person, following what lit my fire, but I still felt like I needed to fit into a world where people mostly did not follow their hearts, where courage was rare. The highs of living a big life at a very young age with a lot of responsibility moved faster than I could keep up with. The good times were great, but I sometimes plunged headfirst into the dark depths of despair. As life moved faster, I was losing sight of who I was.

Then I got pregnant by the man I was dating and finally said yes to his previous proposal of marriage. When my daughter was born, I felt a spark of passion reignite, and I wanted her to know love deeply. I did not have that as a child, and it was what I wanted most.

But the sad reality was that nothing about my life lit my fire anymore. Everything was changed. I kept telling myself that it would work out and to ignore how I truly felt. I was in a very unhappy and unhealthy marriage. I was traveling for work at least twice a month and learned later that I barely knew my husband. Actually, I had no idea who he was. Looking back, I realize I had no idea who I was anymore either. I was working twelve to fourteen hours a day and hardly saw my young daughter. My mother-in-law happily took care of her all day, and she even slept over most nights. I was not taking care of myself—at all—and wore mostly black clothes to cover up all the weight I had gained. I ate fast food late every night after closing my clothing store. It was exhausting, because I had to work long mall hours and interact with hundreds of customers daily.

Around this time, my doctors sent me for some special tests. A few days later, an oncologist was telling me that I had a life-threatening disease. The thought of having limited time here on Earth fired up the yearning to live inside me and rekindled my passion and joy. I made significant changes. The biggest one was getting divorced. My new determination to examine and work on my inner life succeeded, and I got healthy. When the last batch of doctors gave me a clean bill of health, they also announced the news to me that I was pregnant. I had my second daughter a few months after my divorce was finalized and became a devoted single mom. I grew my business again, but moved my retail business online in order to stay home with my girls, and we grew closer. This also gave me time to follow my heart's desire to study holistic medicine, neuroscience, and positive psychology. I've been blessed to have the opportunity to study with some of the leading researchers in these fields.

A few years later, I moved from where I lived in the Caribbean to the U.S. and was swept off my feet by a tall, handsome, blond-haired, and blue-eyed man whom I soon married. This marriage was emotionally void, and once again, without realizing it, my life was dull, without any fire or passion. I felt shrunken and frustrated. Again, I lost my sense of self and meaning. I was always trying to fix the relationship, knowing deep inside I would never be happy with him. But, looking back, I see I just did not know my purpose. So, as I did not have any clarity or direction, I was back in that numb world of "okayness." I knew something was wrong. Something pulled at me, was calling me, and I knew I wanted more—more from life. I had a deep knowing that this could not be *it.*

One day, I was at a conference where I heard someone say that extended heartache occurs when your purpose is not bigger than your pain. That night, I drove to my husband's place to have "the talk." At this point, after so many breakups and makeups, we lived in separate homes. This day was different. We decided it was time to make our divorce official. It was what we both wanted. I looked at him for the last time, then I walked down the staircase and out the door. It was finally final—after years of being on the fence, like a tiring hamster wheel of "Should I go, or should I stay." I learned that I had to let go of the old for something new to be born.

Letting go fully was hard, harder than I could have ever imagined. I felt years of walls around my heart crumble. I suddenly felt the urge to have fun again and realized it had been years. I began to study coaching, and seeing the changes I could make in other people's lives brought new life to mine. I loved traveling—so I did. I was living in Florida at the time but decided to rent a small apartment in Colorado, because I loved it there.

Only a few short weeks after the decision to finally end my marriage for good, I stumbled across the Passion Test book on Amazon. I found out there was going to be a training in Colorado *five minutes* from where I had just rented my apartment. I couldn't believe it!

I attended the Passion Test facilitator certification and felt waves of pure joy intermingled with sadness. I discovered that my number one passion was living with my soul mate in love. In one of the group exercises, I shared that I was fine with ending my marriage, but I felt sad, because I was fearful I would never find true love. Having two divorces behind me made me feel like a failure, and I was terrified that this would be considered an undesirable quality by a future partner. And my second passion was to travel the world (with my soul mate, of course).

My other three passions were that, when my life is ideal,

1. I am fit and healthy,
2. I have financial freedom, and
3. My children are happy and healthy.

Well, faith continued to work its magic, and the beautiful woman next to me at the training put her hand on my shoulder and said with a smile: "I am now on my third marriage, and I can safely say that the third time is the charm. I am madly in love. This is nothing like before. He's here at the hotel with me, and you will see us together for yourself." I was filled with so much hope.

That week, I had a class with my neuroscience professor. I was a student whom he offered one-on-one sessions to because he enjoyed my research so much. He was a wonderful mentor through these major life changes. We talked about my divorce and what was going on for me. I told him that I was clear on my passions, and my number one passion was to be in a lifelong, deep, and committed love. He applauded me for my clarity, admitting that he almost teared up.

I realized during our talk that a lot of my self-talk was about "failing at the marriage" and all the things my husband or I did wrong. Sometimes I would think about all the bad things in that relationship, like how emotionally distant and hurtful it was, and this would make me feel awful. I would get angry at myself for all the years I allowed myself to be treated that way. It hit me during the Passion Test workshop the next day that I was thinking these thoughts over and over; therefore, this was the intention I was setting for myself and my next relationship. During my amicable divorce, I observed that my mind would try to find faults, blame, and regret. So, that night, I grabbed a pad of paper and made a list of all the things I wanted in my next partner, instead of those negative thoughts. I started with things like these:

He brings me flowers
He meditates
He enjoys traveling the world
He owns his own business, like I do
He has a purpose in life
He adores me and is emotionally connected
He considers my feelings and holds them dear
He is at least six feet tall.

I wanted someone who could connect with this new version of myself that was unfolding, so that I would feel loved and cherished. I kept the list in my purse and added to it whenever I caught myself thinking negative thoughts. I practiced mindful awareness and would catch my negativity and choose to think about its opposite instead.

After the Passion Test training, I returned to Florida. I was so crystal clear and simultaneously fully open to intention and surrender. I felt an unmistakable knowing that I needed to move from Florida to Colorado. I had a strong circle of women, and they all told me I was crazy, yet they all supported me. I truly believe that discovering my passions helped me find the courage to finally break down the walls that kept me from true love. I could sense it in a way I could not explain to my friends. I just felt a calling. I knew no one in Colorado... but I had to move *there*. I posted on Facebook that Boulder was calling me like the beating of a drum. I even teared up as I wrote that, my heart so, so full. I had no real reason to move there other than that inner knowing. I had unwavering trust to follow its lead, even though I had no clue where I would wind up. I felt a certainty that I still cannot explain. Since I did the Passion Test so close to my apartment in Colorado, I just knew that I had to go back there... There was something about that place...

Meanwhile, life felt chaotic. My online clothing business was suddenly having trouble, and one of our biggest shipments was lost. One of the professional markers I had set during the Passion Test weekend was that I would fully dive into online group coaching, but I could not find the time while running this other business. I literally looked up at the sky one night and said, "Okay, God, I surrender!" Later that night, a friend messaged me on Facebook to say, "Karen, I think the universe is hitting you with bricks." In my heart, I knew without a doubt that she was right. The chaos in my business felt like a sign.

While I was in Colorado, a dear friend had encouraged me to put up a profile on an online dating site. I had forgotten about it, but just under two weeks before I left Florida, I received an email from a man whose profile said that life was about finding and living a deeper meaning and purpose. I had just given up everything to boundlessly explore purpose and had just gotten the initial design back for my new coaching website, FindingPurpose. com. The universe does not play around. I looked up at the sky once again and thought, *You can't be serious.*

This man and I wrote each other beautiful, lengthy emails for a couple of weeks. They captivated me. We chatted on the phone the week I was in the process of giving away most of my furniture, packing up, and shutting down my business in Florida. He wrote the day before I left, asking if we could meet for a hike. "Sure," I said. *Why not?* I thought.

Just months after taking the Passion Test, I packed up a truck, hired someone to drive my car, and landed in Colorado. Following nothing other than the principles of positive attention and no tension, I somehow wound up right in the arms of my top passion. The day after I landed in Colorado, I met the man who would help unfold the layers of my heart in ways I had no way of knowing needed unfolding. Just his presence made me push through the useless stories that had once held me back. I was not actively looking for love at the time; I was simply in a place of wonder and openness to whatever the divine had in store for me. I had very few expectations and was just happy to begin all over again. Just knowing what lit me up filled me with clarity and purpose, yet I still did not have a plan. I was working out, I felt so alive in the fresh mountain air, and I had so much more energy than when I lived in Florida. By now, I was clear enough to share with him who I was and what I envisioned for my life.

Today, we live and travel together. We still celebrate our love for each other daily, and we are still uncovering how our unique skills and strengths complement each other's. We are each other's mirror. He yearned for more meaning and purpose; I wished for someone to push me past my self-imposed barriers toward love. In the words of T.S Eliot, "The fire and the rose are one."

Hypnotherapist and Strategic Intervention Coach Karen Smith is a woman on a mission to help you discover your purpose. She dares you to be bold, curious, take risks, have faith, see through eyes of hope, and to seek higher wisdom! Her personal belief is that we all have the unlimited ability to create and align with our life destiny and inner knowing. Our work here is to dig beneath the layers that block the flow of our divine intelligence, our connection to source *so we can live the lives we envision and deserve.*

Karen has studied holistic theology, neuroscience, and is currently pursuing a doctorate in natural healing. She brings all those tools and more to her transformational toolkit. From the age of sixteen, she has built several successful businesses from humble and young beginnings, businesses that have positively impacted the lives of thousands of people from every walk of life. Learn more at www.FindingPurpose.com.

Chapter 5

YOU MAKE IT HAPPEN
Deborah (Dee) Redding

*I*s this where I want to be? Am I happy? Do I even know what makes me happy?

2:00 AM. There I was, once again lying awake staring at the ceiling. We had become familiar acquaintances. You would think my brain was on repeat; surely I was watching a rerun. I felt like I was living this scenario a couple of times a week. But this was nothing new. It was a recurring state that I had experienced for years. I'd push past it, getting by, going to work, spending time with family and friends, and experiencing some degree of joy in my life. But something deep inside just wouldn't let me rest. I knew I was fighting a battle that I wasn't going to win, so I decided I needed to listen to that voice, but I didn't know how to get started.

From the outside looking in, I had a great life. People liked me, I was active in my community, and I had great relationships. My career was moving forward. I was employed at a start-up; it was exciting to help build the company from the ground up. I had a good job and a stable income. I was being promoted. I was working hard and feeling confident in what I did. But still, something was missing. I couldn't quite put my finger on it. Ever walk into a room and know that something used to be there that no longer is? That's exactly how I felt. I needed to figure out what was missing and where the heck it had gone.

I walked into work one day. It was a typical day: lots of meetings, a ton to do. I was working on a project and needed some clarity on a few requirements, so I went to see Andreea, a close colleague for the past year. As we went through the details of the project, we talked about some of the challenges that come with building a new business. I decided to share something with her that I hadn't told any of my other colleagues. When I was in my twenties, I had started and sold a successful business, and the idea for the business had come to me one night through a dream. In the dream, I saw myself sitting at my computer selling videos and making a profit. When I woke up, I thought, *That was an interesting dream. Maybe I can do that.* This was when a lot of people were making great incomes by starting businesses on eBay. I wasn't an eBay expert by any means, but I had won a few bids in the past and thought I would see if this was actually something that I could play around with in hopes of making a few extra dollars.

Later that day, I went to a local store that sold used DVDs and video games. The interesting thing is that I'd passed this store many times and never really paid attention to it. But when the idea of selling videos came to me, I knew exactly where I needed to go. I browsed the shelves of titles—some familiar, many not. I came across a DVD box set of *Star Trek: Voyager*. It sparked my interest, perhaps because of the appealing packaging or the fact that everyone is or knows someone who is a huge *Star Trek* fan. I listed the box set as a seven-day auction, with the starting bid at one cent. I was nervous, thinking I was throwing twenty-five dollars down the drain, but I was willing to take a chance. In the end, the set sold for close to ninety dollars! This was the beginning of my online video company. I grew my business and lived off the income for five years. Eventually, I sold it to pursue other things.

As I told Andreea this story, I became filled with so much excitement as I relived it.

I said to her, "I can't believe that happened to me."

Andreea did not skip a beat. "That didn't happen to you," she said. "You made that happen."

Wow, such powerful words. And in that moment, I realized she was absolutely right. I made that happen. I wasn't stopping to recognize what I had made. I had failed to give myself a pat on the back and acknowledge the work that I'd done. We create the lives that we live. Consciously or unconsciously, we attract into our lives the things that we focus on. If I had done it before, surely I could do it again. I just needed to move past what was blocking me and get the energy flowing.

I started with what I knew best. I've always been a big reader and loved inspirational books and quotes. I searched everything from audiobooks to YouTube channels for something that would connect the dots for me. Reading and journaling before bed at night offered some relief and insight. One Sunday, I was casually flipping through channels and I landed on the OWN network. A promotion showed that Jack Canfield, co-author of the successful Chicken Soup for the Soul series, was going to be a guest on today's episode of *SuperSoul Sunday*.

I had heard of Jack and purchased a few of his books over the years, so I was intrigued by what he might have to share with Oprah. Among many interesting things Jack discussed was the Passion Test by his friends Janet and Chris Attwood. I thought, *You mean there is a tool out there that I can use to home in on my passions and incorporate them more into my life? Well, sign me up!* Like many people, I struggled with understanding what my passions were and how to incorporate them into my life. I struggled with balance, and it was taking a toll on me. Sometimes all we need is an arrow pointing us in the right direction. This was my arrow.

I searched online for the Passion Test and ordered the book. The test pushed me to think, to ask myself what was important to me, to look at how I made choices in my life. That is what the Passion Test brought to the table: clarity. Remember those sleepless nights I was having? It hit me that clarity was what I was searching for all along.

I was so busy with the day-to-day—caring for others, being a good friend, sister, daughter, aunt, manager, employee. I found there was a lot of clutter in my mind to sift through. I realized I wasn't always choosing to honor my passions. I was honoring what I thought was necessary, what I thought was important—but why wouldn't my passions be necessary and important? They are.

They're both these things. The truth is I wasn't choosing in favor of my happiness, even though I thought I was. What a lightbulb moment for me. I learned that I have to choose to honor my passions because that *is* choosing happiness. After taking the test, it was clear to me that my passions are the clues to my purpose in life. My passions are important to me, and I need to live what is important to me every day.

My top five passions are

1. Spirit,
2. Connection,
3. Creativity,
4. Family, and
5. Partner.

And the markers helped me identify when I was living my passions. I'm happy to say that being a part of this amazing book was a marker for my spiritual passion, which is centered on connecting deeply with others through support and love. I wanted to touch people and share a story that I knew would help so many people struggling with their purpose and finding their path.

You don't need a bunch of people around you to inspire you, though it can be the spark you need to keep you going. They can remind you that you also have in you what it takes to realize your dreams and live a more passion-filled life. But the thing that really opened my eyes was looking back at all the wonderful things I'd created and the life that I had made. I had created all of this by living life through my passions. I had so many achievements; I had affected and motivated so many lives on a personal and professional level. I listened to myself and created a great business.

When it comes to living a passion-filled life, you've got to do the work; there's no way around that. But just as important is recognizing the work you've done and giving yourself the credit you deserve. How would you feel working a job for twenty to thirty years without ever being acknowledged for any of the contributions you've made? I don't think that would make anyone feel good, nor do I think that motivates you to push higher and higher. The momentum starts to slow, little by little. That is what I was doing to myself, and that is what so many of us do. You have a lot to celebrate. You've built a life, you've made people smile and filled their days with happiness, and you've had fun while doing it. I think that deserves a pat on the back. You don't have to have a lot. Use what you have, no matter how small, to propel yourself out of the darkness and deep into the light.

The Passion Test showed me that I can create a parallel path with what I hunger for internally and what I'm doing daily. It doesn't have to be one or the other. Unfortunately, many of us get to a point where we feel like we have to choose between how we make a living and what brings us happiness. It took courage for me to follow my dreams and own the fact that I am the one who has created this life and who will continue to shape it. I feel more energetic about what's to come every day. I'm more open to the possibilities. I've found that living my life more purposefully, more passionately, equips me with the tools I need to stand strong even in the toughest times.

I struggled a lot with the how—How can this happen? How will I get there?—rather than the doing. Life will have some difficult moments, but it can be fun, awesome, and meaningful. I learned that if I combined what I had to do with what I love to do, it made the tough stuff so much easier. I love being outside, and the feeling of the sunlight on my skin mixed with a cool breeze makes me feel so alive. I took time while writing this chapter to sit out in the sun and make notes about what this experience means to me. To create effortlessly, I was using what I had learned.

You don't have to wait. You can be embodied with intent each day. All you have to do is get started, and you're already well on your way. There will still be times when you may feel confused, trying to understand what you need in order to get where you want to be. But whatever you may be going through, hang in there; you've come too far to give up. Everything will come together, and that will be your confirmation that you're on the right path. You're not reading this by accident. You like the things you like and you're drawn to the people that you are for a reason. Embrace that and live a passion-filled life. Our passions change as we learn and grow, and as our life evolves. The difference is now you will have your own personal tool that will help you through this.

My advice is to read the book, take the Passion Test, and live every day choosing in favor of your passions, in favor of love and happiness. We all need our energy to flow effortlessly. You'll know when you're living your passions; you'll feel it. I've learned that the more I know about myself, the more I get to know myself. The more I know myself, the more happiness I have. Then life is not as much of a struggle. It's the not knowing that leads to struggle.

I've learned to bring the best of myself to each day. I hope this inspires you as much as it has inspired me. The sun was created to support life and provide light, as were you. Just as trees grow to great heights, so were you meant to. Life is a collaboration between you and the universe. You have great things to do.

Deborah (Dee) Redding is an entrepreneur, author, blogger, and senior manager. She is a strong believer in the practice of self-development and awareness, and is committed to leading others through their discovery of self-love, acceptance, and personal fulfillment. She's learned so much about the power of thought and its reflection on our lives, and wants others to experience that same connection. Her mission is to inspire and empower others to live authentically. She always knew she wanted to be a writer and use her gift to inspire others. The oldest of three girls, Deborah was born in Albany, Georgia, and resides in Atlanta. You can follow her on Instagram @journeyofasoul and at www.DeborahRedding.com.

$\mathcal{C}hapter\ 6$

MY UNICORN MADE ME DO IT
Jill Hughes

$\mathcal{D}$o you believe in fairies?

Lately, I've been considering the area where psychology overlaps with metaphysics. Unless we deal with childhood patterns, negative energy, and limiting beliefs, our spiritual growth will always be stunted. Avoiding change and suppressing emotional needs creates an imbalance in our vibrational energy system. Then someone or something has to step in and send us a wake-up call—KA-CHING! In my case it's a fairy godmother and she is not always benevolent, as you'll gather from my story below, sending an illness or an accident that stops me in my tracks, forcing me to pay attention and change direction.

I've experienced plenty of KA-CHINGS! I grew up in Cottingley, an idyllic village in West Yorkshire, England, that is famous for fairies. As you know, in fairy stories there are villains lurking in the forest who snatch little children away and do wicked things to them.

I was four years old when I was abducted outside my grandfather's village bakery shop and abused. Then, at seventeen, I was coming home from an evening out with three of my friends. We'd had a great time and were laughing and joking as we drove down the curved byway on the outskirts of town. Then, as the road narrowed, the car clipped a traffic-calming curb and went into a skid. The driver tried to correct it, but the road conditions were icy. The car was filled with the sound of screaming as it hit a lamppost, crashed through a thick stone wall, turned over, and started to roll.

A day later, I woke up in the hospital to learn that one of my friends had died and one was in intensive care fighting for her life. I spent a while in hospital recovering and, clearly, I was lucky to be alive. But, as I was soon to discover, that was just the beginning.

At twenty-one, I discovered that I had a progressive bilateral condition that resulted in hearing loss. The hearing in my right ear was so bad that several operations were required. Sadly, they didn't fix the problem, so I was left with virtually no hearing, nerve damage, and permanent tinnitus. This actually wasn't very handy, as I worked on the trading floor of an American investment bank. Clearly, I wasn't getting it, so Her Godmotherliness kept upping the ante. On it went: injury, skiing accident, riding accident, illness, cancer, injury, near-death experiences—like a bad horror movie.

Many years and three teenage children later, I found myself in Harley Street, London, the private center of medical excellence, undergoing eye movement desensitization and reprocessing (EMDR) psychotherapy for post-traumatic stress disorder (PTSD). During therapy, I learned about the tendency to be inexplicably drawn to situations that re-create the original trauma. Freud called it the "repetition compulsion."

In his book *Waking the Tiger: Healing Trauma*, Peter Levine refers to this drive as re-enactment, which is a kind of conditioned survival strategy. Levine also highlights the complex and often intriguing recurring accidents, injuries and coincidences that can run a pattern through a traumatized family's history spanning several generations. He cites one family with a member in each of three generations who survived a fatal plane crash—the odds of that happening are pretty staggering. EMDR has been successfully used with Vietnam veterans, and I highly recommend it as a tool to help the brain process distressing memories. It is quite magical.

My Big Wish is that governments worldwide would provide EMDR therapy on demand and automatically upon debriefing of all active service military personnel.

In November 2015, I flew from London to Paris to train to become a Passion Test facilitator. I had left my job in investment banking awhile back and I'd just come through a very difficult and protracted divorce. I felt extremely emotionally bruised and financially diminished, but when an invitation to learn all about the Passion Test pinged into my email inbox, I felt this was my calling and a chance to embrace change.

Onboard the British Airways flight, I felt a combination of excitement and apprehension, as I wondered about the aftermath of the recent ISIL terrorist attacks in Paris where I was headed. Would it be safe? Would there be long delays at the airport due to heightened security?

Midair, I was reading *Ready, Set, Live! Empowering Strategies for an Enlightened Life* on my Kindle when it occurred to me that traumatized individuals, societies, and nations journeying toward a more vital, spontaneous, and joyful life require more than just the alleviation of symptoms. Fundamental shifts and transformation are needed. On a personal level, this was exactly what I hoped the Passion Test would deliver at this stage of my life. Would I be disappointed?

On landing at Charles De Gaulle Airport, things went smoothly right through to the transfer by taxi and checking in at the hotel. In my room, I unpacked and showered. By now, I felt really tired, and although I had taken an "A" level in French in high school, I began to fret how I would cope tomorrow and follow the course material. How on earth would I communicate with the other trainees? Then I saw the lovely gift of sweets and delightful-smelling rose petals with a thoughtful handwritten note that one of our course leaders had left on the desk. I figured it would all work out fine.

Intensive and accelerated learning with love is how I experienced the incredible course. I made some lifelong friends, and although the majority of the attendees were French, it made me realize that hopes, aspirations and passions are universal. We became a family united by passion and all that it encompasses. I discovered that the

Passion Test offers a profound toolkit for change, and for positive empowerment through love and joy.

As you undoubtedly know by now, the Passion Test is a simple yet powerful way to get clear on what matters most to you, and then how to make these passions the priority in your life. Here's what it looked like for me when I discovered that my number one passion is all about wellness:

I have vibrant good health and a joyful abundance of energy.

Marker: People will notice and remark on subtle differences and comment on how relaxed and radiant I appear.

Previously, I never really made my health any kind of priority— the arrogance of youth, I suppose. As we age, consequences catch up with or overtake us, and our health is an issue that comes more into focus. Joints start to ache and creak. Maybe not taking care of yourself also has to do with lack of self-worth, low self-esteem, and putting others first?

With the clarity I gained from The Passion Test, my focus has gravitated toward practices that are beneficial to my health, so I signed up for two online courses with Deepak Chopra— Radical Wellness: Beyond Your Biology and Primordial Sound Meditation.

In Western society, the scientific view of illness is that disease is a random, meaningless event, which is fixed by popping pills and removing body parts or blasting them with radiation. Sadly, the third most common cause of death in the USA is medical/surgical error or malpractice. So I conclude it's better to avoid hospitals, chemicals, and experts in the first place. The body is a conscious energy system, and if it becomes ill, then chances are it's trying to tell us something, so we would do well to look at illness as an opportunity to learn and grow. It's our job to evaluate the message and translate it into action.

Often, ill health is not some form of punishment, karmic debt, or random incident but rather a sign of blockage or imbalance, arising from suppressed emotion. Louise Hay's ground-breaking book on this subject, *You Can Heal Your Life*, is certainly worth a read. Important keys to great health are unconditional self-love and flow—free-flowing ideas and emotions, freely giving and freely receiving love, trusting in the process of life, living in the moment, and practicing positive self-talk. Watch out for negative beliefs that can program illness to develop, such as "I have a family history of type 2 diabetes," or "I go down with the flu every winter."

My partner and I were discussing this metaphysical concept of illness a few weeks after he'd been admitted to the ER with chest pains and an erratic heart rate. His family background is military and undemonstrative—no cuddles from his mom when he was learning to ride a bike and wobbled off, for instance. He's very kind, loving, and supportive, so I didn't quite get why he would manifest a heart problem, which supposedly relates to blockages around giving or receiving love, or losing the ability to feel life's joys. By now, we both knew that the mind, body, and emotions are all connected.

We pondered this until the conversation moved on to how we hold resentment in our bodies. I'd been studying this and advised that the right side is connected with the "masculine" side of the self, the father, and the left side is connected with the "feminine" side, the mother. He concluded that, as the heart is on the left side of the body, there could be a link with the feeling that he hadn't received enough love and support when he was growing up.

This growing realization that all parts of life are connected helped me realize that my #2 passion below is not simply a nice concept but essential to my health and well-being. By clarifying the first passion, I discovered that I could transform my life in ways that support my health and happiness.

How many times have you set aside what you really care about in order to do what you're "supposed" to do? Here's your invitation to follow my lead and change your priorities, too:

I live in a beautiful house near the sea, dreaming of sandy toes and salty kisses.

Marker: Take the Barbados cushion to the new holiday house.

A few months after becoming a Passion Test facilitator, back in the U.K. in the depths of winter, with my body feeling the effects of the cold environment, my passion became increasingly important to me. That's how I plucked up the courage to pack up and move abroad. So now here I am, with an aquamarine swimming pool in the garden that glistens invitingly in the sun, enjoying the benefits of a microclimate thanks to the mountain range and the sea, and reveling in the uplifting effect of the light quality. The seafront promenade that stretches for many long, flat miles beside the ocean is perfect for outdoor activities such as walking, jogging, and cycling.

But what about that cushion?

On last year's holiday to Barbados, my daughters packed light. I, however, did not and was way over the limit on the way there. Ouch, a hefty surcharge bit. And this did not bode well for the collection of shells, driftwood, seaweed, blow-up plastic unicorn balloons from the carnival, tablecloths and napkins, carved wooden mermaid, porcelain sea horses, and hand-carved oil drum top (yes, oil drum!) on the way home, now did it? Then there was the *Sandy toes, Salty Kisses* cushion that I was determined to bring home with me.

"Mum, it's impossible. Leave it!" the girls wailed, as I got redder and redder in the face trying to zip my suitcase.

"No way," I replied through gritted teeth. "Girls, just sit on it!"

They did, and now here it is, taking pride of place in the new holiday house. For all the extra trouble the cushion is now a treasured memory of the trip and a powerful connection to this passion. And it's a clear marker that I'm on track with focusing on my passions first and foremost.

Of course, sometimes my daughters look at the cushion and shake their heads in disbelief.

"Mum, you are, like, a bit crazy, though, aren't you?"

"Sure," I reply laughing, "but you know what? My unicorn made me do it."

My number three passion:

I'm studying and growing with spiritual masters and supported by enlightened mentors.

Ever since I attended Denise Linn's Past Lives workshop several decades ago, I have believed that I was a sorcerer in Gnostic times, and subsequently a witch, so I'm quite into herbs for healing and plant-based solutions. Indeed, my lovely daughters indulge such notions, no doubt with the odd nudge-nudge-wink-wink when I'm not looking. However, they are not so tolerant of the five bean and turmeric casserole that's bubbling away on the stove.

One lifts the lid and peers inside: "What's that? I hope you don't think we're going to eat this stuff."

"Well—" *tread carefully here*, I think to myself, *not too much jargon* "—did you know that beans mean health?"

"Really?" The eldest one arches an immaculately threaded eyebrow. "That sounds like a Heinz advert."

"No," the youngest says, shaking her head, "worse than that. She's having another Harry Potter moment!"

As you can see a side benefit of passion number three is not being concerned about what others think about me, including my beloved daughters. Just as important, clarity about this passion has helped me put my deepening understanding of life at the forefront of my priorities and that in turn has given me a rich treasure of experiences to serve as the basis of passion number four.

Passion four is as follows:

I achieve international fame and recognition thanks to the phenomenal success of my self-help book.

This chapter is my first step towards realizing that passion. That book—*Money: Stop Worrying About It and Start Pulling It to You*—is still a work in progress. Initially, I was surprised to find myself writing about money, even though I'm highly qualified as a former investment banker, foreign exchange spread betting trader, and property developer.

In Paris in 2015, at the same time as the deep wounds from the terrorist atrocities were still healing, world leaders arrived to discuss climate change and come up with the architecture to tackle the emissions problem. The outcome of this delegation and global agreement will attract financial flows into green energy. Already, Bill Gates is teaming up with other billionaires to get innovative solutions out of the lab. Clearly, solving this global issue requires money. For me, creating wealth is essential to people like you and me who are committed to positive change in the world.

Before I took the Passion Test, I thought I would write a book about life purpose, but one of the things I learned about myself while training in Paris was that I had a number of limiting beliefs about the relationship between spiritualism and money, and about selling in particular. Chris and Jessica, our amazing master trainers, helped me shift these beliefs, and I came to realize that people can't self-actualize to higher levels if they are worrying about money on a day-to-day basis.

So herein I found my true calling.

Finally, here is my last passion:

I am dancing under the stars, listening to the music of my soul.

I hope my story shows you just how powerful the Passion Test has been in helping me get aligned with my life purpose. And it can be just as powerful for you. Remember, it's the journey, and not the destination, that matters. Isn't it better to release struggle and trauma and grow through love and joy? That's what the Passion Test offers. This might seem like an easy option, but it requires you to expand, to embrace challenges, to change, and to follow your inner guidance.

Because I'm now committed to growth through love and joy, I invested in a CD of Gregorian chanting: I play this amazing music in the car–often and loudly. However, as it is not everyone's cup of tea, invariably there's a unified chorus of moaning from the backseat.

"Mum, please! Not the darn GREGORS again!"

Amen?

P.S. My unicorn made me do it.

Jill Hughes spent twenty-three years working in investment banking at the sharp end, both in London and on Wall Street. She built up a property portfolio with her former husband, since sold because of divorce, which she's rebuilding from scratch. She has three children: an Aquarian, a Pisces, and a likewise Libra. The family's three Houdini dogs adore shredding beds; devouring stuffed hedgehogs; barking at Zilla (Godzilla), the transgender cat; eating fences; playing at shed Olympics; and keeping Joseph, the resident carpenter, pretty busy. Jill has an Honours degree in English, creative writing, and film. She trained with Coach U and is a qualified and experienced TEFL instructor and Passion Test facilitator. Jill is one of the U.K.'s top wealth mentors and hopes you'll visit her website soon: www.moneymagnet.global.

Chapter 7

NOT JUST ANOTHER YEAR
Ulrike Berzau

*A*nother year of strategic planning," I sighed. It felt like scaling a big mountain. I just wasn't excited about going through the routine again of figuring out and setting next year's goals. I just wasn't that inspired. Maybe you've been in that same position.

But if I, the executive leader, wasn't enthusiastic about the process, how could I expect my team to be inspired? Out of my own frustration, I discovered the key to making moments like these transformational and you may also find it can transform dreariness to excitement in your own world.

I didn't want this process to affect me that much because I did enjoy leading my hospital, a 102 bed rehabilitation hospital with multiple ambulatory sites. We offered specialized services for patients with brain injuries, spinal cord injuries, stroke and other conditions across the whole age range, from the toddler beginning the journey of life to the fragile elderly hanging on to physical function. Our hallways, patient rooms and gymnasiums were filled with activity, one could see therapists encouraging patients to take a step, cheering on the ones who lost hope and providing compassionate care for every patient and their families.

When I reflected on the importance of our services and dedication of my staff, suddenly the coaching training I'd gone through came to my mind. How could I forget? I'd learned how to set goals that truly inspire, goals that stimulate us to stretch above and beyond, and goals that take us out of our comfort zone. Only those types of goals lead to inspired actions.

It was time to put this into action and it took some courage. I didn't know how my team would respond. At our next Executive Leadership Team meeting I surprised them by asking the questions:

What gets you really excited about your work?

How would you like to see the hospital moving forward?

What is your vision for your department?

What is your BIG goal?

What are you passionate about?

Still today, I can see the look on their faces and feel the moment of silence in the boardroom when I started asking the questions. A bit puzzled and wondering where I was going, five of the nine executives started to engage. It was fascinating to hear their ideas and big vision and it was contagious. Very soon everyone participated and the sparkles in their eyes as each shared their vision for their departments and services was truly inspiring.

The enthusiasm grew and we decided to move this forward. I asked them to present their managers and staff with the same questions and encourage the managers to share their vision and BIG goal at the hospital wide leadership meeting.

Within a short time, there was such an excitement in the hospital, people were smiling and connecting, talking about things they wanted to do, and sharing their goals and vision. In the following months, we came up with an exciting strategy.

Our strategy was built on what we all felt matters most to achieve exceptional outcomes for our patients. It was built on what was truly important to increase engagement and loyalty in our employees and what matters most to our hospital's accomplishments. We changed processes, realigned work and created new opportunities to allow team members to use their unique gifts and talents to more effectively contribute to the success of the hospital.

Our vision, to be the "internationally renowned rehabilitation institute achieving exceptional outcomes" was posted all over, each meeting agenda had it written on the top.

You can't imagine the excitement and joy I saw in my staff's eyes when in less than a year, we received amazing news: We were awarded the Hospital of Choice Award Top 10 in the nation!

Today, I realize we achieved this award because we followed the principle of giving priority to "what matters most." Though I was unaware of the Passion Test or the Passion Test for Business at the time, I later discovered this is at the core of what may consider "the #1 tool for discovering passion and connecting with purpose."

My Journey

My personal Passion Test journey began when I decided to leave my hospital executive position. After a rewarding and successful career as a healthcare executive leading rehabilitation services and hospitals, I shifted my focus to follow my entrepreneurial spirit. Over the years, I had the opportunity to learn from the world's best in the personal development area—mind, body, and spirit— and I wanted to apply the spectrum of my skills and experiences to benefit others.

I started with the following vision for my coaching and consulting business: I am passionate about leading individuals, teams, and organizations to exceptional results in life and business.

Coaching and consulting became my chosen full-time work. I thought it was what I wanted to do, but after a short time, I felt stuck. My title changed when I left the hospital world, but my mental programming had not. My subconscious was still set on being the hospital CEO and had no frame of reference for being a successful coach.

I was unsure how to advance and grow my business, and I became frustrated. Then one of my coaching colleagues told me about the Passion Test. It sounded interesting and timely, as I'd lost my excitement for and confidence in what I was doing.

I signed up for the Passion Test facilitator certification course but canceled a few months later because of a time conflict. Thankfully, at the last minute, I decided to make it a priority and re-enrolled. Taking that course was quite an experience, and I fondly remember when Karin Lubin, our master trainer, took me through the test. I realized I wasn't living my passions. For example, my top passion—spending more fun times with my son, Moudy, and his then-fiancée and now-wife, Carrie—was not really present in my life. I lived on the West Coast and they lived in Brooklyn, New York. I missed out on being close to the most important people in my life.

Likewise, my other top passions—enjoying freedom with an abundance of time and money, enjoying nature and horses, riding dressage, and leading others to exceptional results—were not present in my life to the extent I wanted them to be. And I wasn't taking action to move closer to living my passions either. I knew that passions are the catalyst to inspired actions, and actions lead to results. It was time to make a change.

Three months after I took the Passion Test, I moved to the greater New York area. Now I see the newlywed couple for brunch in the city and they come to visit me. Also, I found the most amazing riding stable, Knightsbridge Farm, where I'm pursuing my equestrian passion and truly enjoying every moment of it.

My life started to blossom, but what about my business?

Being Two People

Have you ever felt like you were two people? For example, you have a day job, and you also have your own business or hobby on the side where you pursue a dream, passion, or interest?

I've always enjoyed leading rehabilitation services and hospitals, and I was good at it, yet I was ready for more. Something in me drove me to more—more freedom, variety, impact—and new ventures.

Interestingly, I felt rather vulnerable as I focused solely on my new coaching and consulting business. When I looked at my business' growth, I worried about my decision. It's a very common worry—we tend to measure our results only by the financial outcome, and when we don't see it happening, we focus more and more on it and get more and more worried. My worry was a sign I was getting emotionally involved with the lack of success and unwanted outcomes; thus, I created more of the same. One of the powerful principles I'd learned when I took the Passion Test course was, *Whatever you focus your attention on grows stronger in your life.* I was seeing it clearly in my lack of income growth.

I decided enough was enough. I understood the powerful concept of Intention, Attention, No Tension and knew how the mind works. We are programmed to measure our effectiveness by what we see, typically in numbers. When we look at our company results, we focus on the financials and volume— for example, the number of clients/customers, sales, or profit margin. We look at our success through these numbers and allow them to determine whether we're having a good or bad month or year. All of these negative thoughts just bring more of the same—more of the results we don't want. Whatever you give your attention to grows, and your thoughts become your reality. And I was putting most of my attention on what I didn't want, instead of what I did want.

During the Passion Test course, we learned to look at our challenges as gifts—voilà, a new idea was born. Instead of looking at the lack of clients and profit, I started to look at my businesses holistically and "met with myself" weekly to review my progress in all areas. I looked at the quality of the services I provided; the results my clients achieved; my development, advancement, and creativity; the visibility and recognition I gained; the relationships I built; and whether I pushed myself beyond my comfort zone. All these were important areas, and financial success and the number of clients became only two of the many measures of success.

I shared this approach with my clients and fellow coaches and encouraged them to think about how many areas their business affects every day and to redefine their success measures. I learned a valuable lesson, and now I could help others. I even published a free ebook, *Key Measures of Success*.

My Coaching and Consulting Business

As I mentioned earlier, my top business passion has been leading individuals and organizations to achieve exceptional results, and I felt I had a good start with my executive experience and coaching, but I hadn't reached my potential. There was more to achieve, much more.

As part of the Passion Test practice builder mentoring program, I experienced the Passion Test for Business and, with my strategist Beth Lefevre, developed an incredible strategy for my coaching and consulting business. I felt inspired and had a road map for my company, goals based on what's most important to me, and action items to achieve them. Curious about this powerful process and eager to learn more, I signed up for the Passion Test for Business certification course. It all clicked for me there. I could see that discovering your business' passions and priorities is the catalyst for your success. The process brought me clarity, and I realized I not only had a plan for my business, but also a process to transform other businesses and achieve my vision of leading individuals and organizations to exceptional results.

What Sets a Business Apart?

One important part of the Passion Test for Business is defining the Unique Contribution that sets a company apart from others in the marketplace and industry.

While going through this process, I suddenly realized what makes me unique. I could build on my past successes as a healthcare executive and leader of executive teams with my coaching and consulting skills, education, and new experiences, instead of being "two different people," as I had felt for years.

I witnessed many of my coaching colleagues being stuck. They developed their coaching business and still had a day job, keeping two identities and not moving forward by aligning their unique skills and gifts. Even when they began coaching full time, their business did not take off and blossom. With the Unique Contribution, I found a way to tie it all together, building on my strengths and letting my uniqueness shine.

Have you thought about what makes you unique? What are the unique skills, gifts, talents, and experiences you bring to the world and your life, career, and business? Instead of fitting in and doing what everyone else does, let your uniqueness shine. Only you have certain gifts, and only you can bring your purpose to the world.

Wouldn't you agree the greatest inventions and advances came from those who built on their unique skills and talents? When you become more of who you are, you become irresistible and attract the right people in your life. You let the world know what you stand for and your values. In your business, you attract the team that thrives in your environment and customers who are attracted to you because of your company values.

A great example is Tony Hsieh's company, Zappos. He shares his company's values in his book, *Delivering Happiness,* and the mission is clear: "To live and deliver WOW."

Developing a Strategy

The other important piece of the Passion Test for Business is developing a strategy based on what matters most to the entrepreneur, executive leaders, employees, company's success, and customers. This strategy is based on the values, passions, and priorities of the business. Wouldn't it be amazing if all businesses based their strategies on the passions of their leaders, employees, and company? Imagine how inspired the workforce would be. Wouldn't you want to have a strategy for your company, division, or department that is based on what matters most and to enjoy the innovation, excellence, and productivity of an inspired workforce?

Through the Passion Test for Business process, I developed a clear road map based on what truly mattered to me and my business. My top business passions speedily became a strategy when I added markers and action steps. Similar to the Passion Test for Life, in the Passion Test for Business you identify markers to keep you on track, like road markers and signs tell you that you're on track toward your destination. This process becomes a powerful strategy, a roadmap to success—for entrepreneurs, business owners, small companies, or large organizations— because the Passion Test transforms a business' culture. Identifying what matters most to the leaders and employees in all aspects of their work is the catalyst for goal-achieving actions. Actions lead to results.

Employee Engagement—Work and Core Passions

During my career as a hospital executive, we frequently conducted employee engagement surveys and worked on improving the scores. Often, we worked so hard on engagement but didn't see the survey results improve. We wondered what else we could do, but the truth is you can't improve how people feel. You can only create an environment where people can grow and blossom, use their unique skills, and follow their passions.

Did you know, according to Gallup studies, almost 70 percent of the American workforce is disengaged? People are unhappy, unsatisfied, and unfulfilled. This affects company profits and customer relations. Interestingly and sadly, disengaged employees report almost double the number of "unhealthy" days—days when health issues limited their activity—as engaged employees. All of this costs the U.S. economy billions in lost productivity each year. It doesn't have to be that way (Harter & Adkins, Gallup, 2015).

In 2015 *Harvard Business Review* published a study by Garton & Mankins, showing that engaged employees produce nearly 1.5 more than average employees, and inspired employees produce 2.25 times more.

I was fascinated to learn that when we apply the Passion Test to companies with employees, we go a step further and work with the employees to identify their work and core passions. The comprehensive Passion Test for Business process and Culture Action Plan allow us to align employee needs and goals with company goals and uniquely position the business in the market.

Imagine work being a place where people enjoy what they're doing, can fully express their gifts and talents, and contribute to the company's success and the advancement of products and services.

Through the Passion Test for Business process, we transform businesses by bringing out individuals' unique skills and passions. We develop an action plan that produces lasting results—increased productivity, innovation, engagement, excellence, growth, profitability, and sustainability.

As of today, I have witnessed many remarkable transformations using the Passion Test for Business process. I love the story of one of my clients. While writing this chapter, I just got her call, "I reached my goal and it's all because of you and your Passion Test." Of course I remembered her goal because it's quite audacious and I remember the many times she shared how much it means to her to take **three months vacation each year to travel and enjoy**! Travel for her is not a road trip, her trips are extensive overseas journeys filled with exciting activities and family visits abroad.

When we started to work together on her business she was struggling to make payroll and now she's financially able to take three months off. Plus, she joyfully said during our call (and I could feel the big smile in her voice) "I bought a business class ticket for my next trip." Her business has now grown to 50 employees and eight locations with increasing revenue to allow her the lifestyle she wants. She shared with me: "I learned to identify and set my goals, personally and professionally, consistent with what matters most to me, **my values and my passions**. This helped me to see things from a different perspective, free myself from unnecessary stress and brought clarity to my plans for the future, much more than if I would have tried to do it on my own. Today I am **focused, calm**

and confident. I am excited about my progress and am confident about the continued growth and success for me personally and for my company."

My Business Passions

For my own business as I mentioned, my number one business passion is leading individuals and organizations to achieve exceptional results. Let me share with you just a few of my other top business passions:

1. My company is highly respected and sought after as the leader in business transformation.
2. We have a network, a team of exceptionally talented and capable people providing outstanding services.

How did I do on those? Having a global impact and working with others always inspired me, and I was clear on my passions, markers, and actions. My business passions led me to become the national account manager of the Passion Test for Business. Here I have a global impact, and I'm working with a team of exceptional people.

It's amazing how things align!

Now, you might wonder, What's number three? Here it is:

3. We publish incredible, transformational, innovative, and inspiring books and programs that generate income while we sleep, play, or work.

My dear reader, my passion led me to be part of this inspiring book with *New York Times* best-selling authors, and I hope it will be transformational for you as you find your passion in life and in business.

Ulrike Berzau, MM, MHS, PT, FACHE, is passionate about leading individuals, teams, and organizations to achieve exceptional results. She has extensive experience as a healthcare executive, received many leadership and quality awards, and led two hospitals to being recognized with the Hospital of Choice Award, one even in the top ten in the nation. Ulrike is the co-author of the international bestseller Imagine a Healthy You, *an executive certified coach and consultant, and the national account manager for the Passion Test for Business/ASAP Engagement Consulting. She holds master's degrees in management and in health science, physical therapy, and is a fellow of the American College of Healthcare Executives. Her website is www.ulrikeberzau.com.*

Chapter 8

A BILLION PASSIONATE PEOPLE
LIVING MAGNIFICENT LIVES

Shivani Gupta

ust after September 11, I trekked through the Annapurna range in Nepal. As everyone else had canceled their trip, it was the first time in many years that I had time to feel and think, and not talk. Little kids ran up to me and said hello, as often this was the only English word they knew. Their enigmatic smiles left a mark on my heart. One family invited me into their hut, where there was only enough room for five people to sit. I was the sixth. They prompted me to sit down as the mother served the meal. She took the five plates and from each took away a small amount of rice and put it on a sixth plate for me. They smiled. They were content. I had so much yet felt empty and like I needed more, like a dry well.

In the villages of Nepal, I encountered some of the poorest families, yet they smiled and invited me to share their small meals, often without knowing where their next meal was coming from. They seemed content when I shared with them a little candy that cost me about one cent. The contentment they felt was miles from what I felt.

I was at a career high, with a degree in engineering, an MBA, and a very well-paid senior executive position for a global firm. I was traveling business class and negotiating deals. However, I was finding it increasingly hard to maintain the long hours and, despite the money, was finding it hard to stay motivated at work. I was also in a relationship that had lost its mojo.

During that month, I slowly got rid of the layers that were constricting me and figured out my "why." I came back from my trip and knew I had to do things differently. I took radical steps, as I was not sure I would have the courage to do little tasks each week. I quit my job and my relationship. The "why" I discovered in Nepal was to create a billion passionate people living magnificent lives.

Learning the Universe Delivers

"Passion" is not a word that has always been associated with business. Thankfully, that has changed in the last few years. It is often passion that inspires people to start a business in the first place. Many people are passionate about their craft or about being their own boss. They want to do things a particular way, not just from a point of control but to make a positive change in other people's lives or in their own.

I often felt guilty for loving my work, because I'm a woman, a mother, and have an Indian background, which means none of the women in my family have worked. I was both riddled with guilt and filled with relief when I first did the Passion Test in 2011 and discovered that my number one passion is work.

Because I realized that work is my number one passion, and my "why" is creating a billion passionate people living magnificent lives, I knew my work had to be meaningful. I created markers for that passion. I wanted to help and influence more people to find and activate their passions and reduce their stress. I also realized to do that I didn't have to take everyone to Nepal.

I brainstormed how I could influence people without always spending my own time. I made a list of other businesses I could run and direct without sacrificing my time as a speaker and mentor—which would be limited if I wanted to reach a billion people. The list included my passions: a day spa, a yoga studio, a food outlet, and something to do with kids.

Three weeks (yes, three weeks!) after doing the Passion Test, I was getting my monthly massage with the owner at my local spa and she started to tell me how she was going to sell the business. Forgetting at the time that a spa was on my list (duh!), I started offering her ideas for how she could avoid selling and still make money. At the end of the conversation, she asked, "Why don't you buy it?" I thought this was a silly idea—until that night when I got home and saw the note with the list I had written. I began to cry. It happened so fast!

My BIG learning as I have experimented with the Passion Test is that the universe (you can replace this with any other word that resonates with you) delivers what you need when you get clear on your "why" and your passions.

I bought the spa and set up a second one in a busy shopping center. The business now has twenty-seven staff, a large turnover, and a great profit. And I manage it in less than four hours a week.

Hanging around with Like-Souled People

I believe setting goals in areas you aren't passionate about is a waste of time. I learned from the Passion Test to get clear on which passions I was going to focus on this year, or in a defined period, and then set the SMART (specific, measurable, achievable, realistic, and in a time frame) goals in that area. For example, "I want to lose weight" is not a SMART goal. But "I want to lost ten pounds in the next twelve weeks" is.

There are two key questions I ask myself to stay connected to my number one passion, my work:

1. What projects in the business am I passionate about?
2. What can I outsource, delegate, or delete that I'm not passionate about?

However I looked at it, it always came down to seven areas of passion:

Work

Family

Money

Friends
Spirit
Body
Mind

I arrange these seven areas of passion into a hierarchy each year and work out which three I'm going to master. I know I can only master three and do the other four at an average level.

When I did the hierarchy of passions in 2003, friends were last. This doesn't mean I'm a bad friend. In fact, I'm a loyal friend who has kept some relationships for more than twenty-five years. I have lots of friends in different work and personal circles. We want to associate with passionate people in our personal and professional lives, as we're the sum of the people we surround ourselves with. When I did the Passion Test, I realized there were some people in my life—friends, family, and some clients—who didn't serve my passion. What this highlighted for me was that I was saying yes to a lot of things my friends were asking of me that were not in my top passions, then feeling like I had little time to live my passions, and feeling resentful as a result. Can you relate?

I needed to make some changes. I decided to get clear on the people I was hanging around with. I made a conscious choice to not hang around with people who appeared to have similar values and passions on the surface, but underneath, their DNA was different. They were lovely to my face but draining me energetically. I decided to minimize my contact with people in some areas and gently cut other people out of my life. I called this "hanging around with like-souled people."

The Passion Test cleared my energy levels, my time levels, and my guilt levels. As I met new friends, I came across my markers in the form of friends who had similar values and passions, and that has increased the flow of my energy into other areas that are high on my passion list.

Leaving Guilt Behind

When family came second in my hierarchy of passions in 2003, and then again in 2008 after my first child was born, I felt guilty. I had a lot of baggage around this. I was brought up in a culture where women were educated, but once they were married, they looked after their children. I am the first woman in my lineage to work. I knew I had to. For myself and my daughter. I knew it was better for me and also better for her. However, with it came judgment from my family and friends, who asked, "Why are you going back to work when she is only six weeks old?" But the Passion Test helped me realize that it's not that I'm not available for my family or that I wouldn't be there in a flash if they needed me. It just means that I can focus on my work and live my "why" without feeling guilty.

I can appreciate why I wanted to go back to work six weeks after giving birth. I had wanted a baby since the age of twenty, and when I had my daughter at thirty-six, and then my son at thirty-seven, I loved them and wanted to be with them as much as I could. But I also had a yearning to get back to work. Not out of financial need or out of fear, but out of love. I love my work. It's my number one passion.

When I start to feel guilty about work now (I still feel guilty sometimes but nowhere near as much as I did before I did the

Passion Test), I ask myself, "How many people am I helping? What would I rather feel on my deathbed?"

I try to manage everything in thirty-five hours or less each week, and I engage my kids in my work. When they ask me about my day, I don't just say, "It was good." I tell them what I did, what I loved, and what I didn't enjoy. This creates a lively conversation and encourages them to talk about school and sports in as much detail.

Activating Passion in Business

In 2011, I decided to become a Passion Test facilitator with Janet Bray Attwood. After the training, I started to work with people in defining their top five passions. I dedicated myself to helping leaders find and activate passion in their businesses. I had an opportunity to work with a leader who ran an organization of about three hundred people. He was very unhappy and took his frustrations in life out on his employees. When we did his passions, his top passion was to jam on his guitar with his high school buddies. At forty-eight years old, he was overweight. He worked around sixty hours a week. He did not feel connected to his family or his music. We spoke about him jamming in his garage once a week to activate his passion. This simple exercise got his life more connected to his passions.

Here are my seven steps to getting passionate about your business:

1. Understand and unlock your passion as a business owner or leader.

2. Understand the passions of your staff and align them to your business goals.
3. Give your passion purpose.
4. Communicate the "why" of your business to your staff in their language.
5. Use vision boards to help you and your team get clear about purpose.
6. Create a values-driven culture in your business.
7. Maintain balance in your life to maintain passion.

Unlocking your passion today is a great first step toward a more prosperous and rewarding career and a more productive business. It will help you set and achieve goals in your life, career, or business. Ask yourself what you're passionate about and how you can regain lost passion for your business or trade.

Knowing what you and your staff are passionate about is really important, but it isn't everything. I meet many people who have lots of passion but are lost. In business, and in your personal life, passion needs to align with a very important factor. You need purpose for your passion. Without purpose, your passion has no soul. If passion is the vehicle, purpose is the fuel. Passion without a purpose is like having a fast car with nowhere to go.

My business success has come from aligning my passion to a purpose of helping others to be more passionate and productive. I have established a purpose to be a beacon for others to find their passion. My purpose is being a "passion activator." An example of putting purpose to my passion is the fundraising leadership tours to India I run. They combine two passions of mine: helping alleviate poverty and abuse among Indian girls, and inspiring people. The trips help leaders be better by allowing them to reflect on their passion and purpose.

Asking why purpose is important answers the question. Your business purpose is your overarching "why." Why are you in business or in your role? Focusing on your "why" helps inform decision-making and ensures the small things add up to something bigger.

Your "why" is your business vision. Vision boards are an effective tool that I use for myself and for my clients. Cut out pictures of the things you would love to manifest in your business or life and put them on a board or computer screen. Vision boards are particularly useful for people who are visual and get bogged down by writing a vision statement. You are articulating your dreams and hopes. You are getting clear on what you are passionate about in your business or life and what you are trying to achieve.

A vision should be inspirational, stand the test of time, and express your passion. Think BIG and look ahead! Here is a checklist of questions to test your current or new vision:

Is it precise, practical, and achievable?

Is it forward-thinking?

Does it describe what you really believe in and want?

Is it compelling?

The beginning of a new year is a good time to reexamine passion and purpose, but regular check-ins ensure what you are doing is in alignment with the big picture.

If your staff know the purpose of the business (the strategy, the vision, and the mission), they can align their passion to it. Leaders can engage their employees in a way that harnesses passion. People naturally want to know why they should do things. We often spend time telling staff and customers how to do things, but we fail to take them with us on why a business is on a certain path.

Here are my three tips for activating your passion to help the people in your business activate theirs:

1. Take the time to understand your people's passions.
2. Don't judge other people's passions.
3. Try to align your business's brand with the passions of the individuals within it.

Creating a values-driven culture is another way to speak to employees' passions. Successful organizations and entrepreneurs keep their business values front and center. By asking staff to think about how their actions or ideas reflect the business's values, positively or negatively, you can create a culture or purpose to which passion can align. The more you talk about values and purpose, the more it gives permission for other people to talk about them as well. It is a constructive way to enable staff to talk about anything and makes tough conversations easier, too.

Not having the right work-life balance is a passion killer. Many business owners and leaders I work with have lost their passion because they're feeling burnt out—by too much work, by employee demands. There is a very good reason why an airline safety demonstration tells you to put your own oxygen mask on before helping others. You can't be a passionate leader and help your staff to be passionate if you are not taking care of yourself. You won't have the energy or passion to create new ideas in your business.

Use a holiday to switch off from work. Some downtime with family and friends is important to recharge. And recharging is good for business. Think of it as working on the business rather than in it. Some reflection when recharging is also beneficial. Think about what worked well for you this year and what you don't want to repeat next year. Don't make it onerous. What has fueled your passion this year and what is killing it? Do more of the former and decide on one thing you can do to stop the latter.

Finding my passions has allowed me to achieve success. I run a number of businesses that employ more than fifty staff. My passions have also given me the energy to write numerous books and become a certified professional speaker. My work has been published in five countries and two languages. The successes from the Passion Test continue in all areas of my life. In 2016, I committed to working with Janet on her Design Your Enlightened Life program to deepen my understanding of how I can dive further into my own passions, and then as a result help others do the same.

However, passion on its own is not enough. You need to live the Passion Test and constantly review it to make a difference for yourself and others. I do the Passion Test every year on January 1, and so do my husband and my five- and seven-year-old kids. It is a ritual in our family that we love. Although the kids are young, they're starting to realize that when you do the Passion Test, your life becomes clearer. If you have not done the Passion Test, do not waste a moment. When you are clear on your passions, the universe is waiting to deliver. Here's to your passion!

Shivani Gupta is the Passion Activator. The founder and chief passion officer at Passionate People Institute is a former Young Businesswomen of the Year. She's also an author, speaker, workshop facilitator, and mentor. She has the keys to the Passion Map, Leadership Map, Communication Map, and Freedom Map to help inspire, challenge, and transform you to achieve business and personal success and fulfillment. Shivani is a certified professional speaker (CSP) whose keynotes and workshops will activate your passion in an engaging and practical way. One of Shivani's passions is helping impoverished girls receive the education they deserve. She is an ambassador for Barefoot College and supports this worthy charity with proceeds from her work. Connect with Shivani at www.askshivani.com.

Chapter 9

YOU CAN DO ANYTHING!
MY TRIUMPH OVER
DOMESTIC VIOLENCE

Veronique Scheldeman

I was born in Belgium in January 1969, the fruit of a stressful, self-serving, and conditional love. My mom wished for two boys, and I was the second of two girls. My sister and I grew up the hard way. My parents had a unique dynamic, more of a love-hate relationship, punctuated by a lot of domestic disputes. My father was high-handed with my mom. During domestic disputes, my parents wouldn't address each other directly, so my sister and I served as mediators to pass on the messages. My mom was very critical of us. We had to be very fast when responding to her. She would count to three, and if we didn't act, we got a spanking. As a result, I lived in fear of my parents for thirty years, afraid to ask for anything.

When I was six years old, I met a girl who became my childhood best friend, Cecile Baguette. She was the fourth in a family of six children, with one adopted—her brother next to her in age, who was from India. Her maternal grandmother was physically disabled from having polio as a child and sewed socks for those in need. Cecile's mother was a housewife and a volunteer in a grade school. She was very active in the community and collected clothes and useful items for a clinic in Madagascar. I told my mom that all the clothes that were too small for us should go to the Baguette family to send to Madagascar, where they could be useful for other children. I regularly carried suitcases full of items from my place to Cecile's, which was about two hundred yards away. I learned a lot from this family—about adoption, disabilities, sharing, and helping people. They gave me a warm welcome and treated me like one more child in the family. They loved me unconditionally.

When I was seven years old, I knocked at my neighbor's door by mistake when I came out of the elevator in our apartment building. Our neighbor was an old, childless woman from Luxembourg named Miss Neuman. She had been a baker and made delicious sugar tarts. Anytime I visited her, she prepared blanched almonds—her specialty. She became like a grandmother to me. And my bond with her taught me how to have relationships with seniors.

At the age of seven and a half, my paternal grandmother taught me to drink milk, because until then I drank only water. I was very small for my age, and she thought I needed to drink milk to grow stronger. I didn't like milk, and it was difficult for my body to digest it, but she told me many times: if you want, you can do anything!

These words are my strongest belief today and the one thing that permits me to overcome my fears and obtain what I desire in life.

When I was between nine and twelve, my parents moved my sister and me to a different school without discussing it with us. We were sent to a boarding school about sixty miles from our home. We left by train on Monday morning and returned Friday night. Living in the dormitory was difficult for me because it was only for girls and I was a tomboy. I suppose my mom hoped to make me more feminine. There was a girl in my class who bullied me—and she was also staying in the dorm. We all know how nasty children can be to each other, and I had no one to protect me. Fortunately, she left the school after the first year. Despite all the pain she caused me, I believe in unconditional love and can't hate her.

My last year at boarding school was my last year of elementary school. I was the only one in my class who was a resident. My teacher didn't call me by my name; she called me *"pupuce,"* which means flea, because I was so small. It took a lot of courage for me to put my hand up when the teacher asked us to bring something to class the next day and I knew I couldn't because I lived in the dorm.

That's all I remember of my childhood.

My adolescence went quite smoothly. I was a quiet girl and didn't make waves at home. My sister was more rebellious and created a lot of conflict between her and my parents, and I was left alone to support them.

As for my love life: unfortunately, it mirrored that of my parents. My first boyfriend, whom I met while doing my management studies, was a tyrant, not with me so much but with his mom and his sister, and I realized that he wasn't a good man for me.

In March 1998, I married a man who was very nice in the beginning but who I would later discover had stalked his previous girlfriend. I didn't know that his mom was an alcoholic and that his father had raised him.

I didn't want to see his true nature.

We had three daughters together: Marie, who is seventeen years old; Lauraline, who is sixteen; and Louise, who is eleven. Three months after Marie's birth, my husband became depressed and started drinking. In 2004, I discovered I was paying for his alcohol and decided to stop buying it. I realized I was enabling his alcoholism and resolved to leave him. That was when the verbal abuse began and I became his scapegoat.

In 2007, we separated and I gained full custody of my daughters, but his harassment didn't stop. In December 2008, I was burned out as a result of daily personal and professional stress. So I asked the courts to place my daughters with their father for a few months so that I could get treatment. But this backfired, and my ex-husband got full custody of the girls. He forced my daughters to say that they never wanted to see me again. It was very hard for me, and I had to get better as soon as possible.

For twelve years, I suffered emotional and economic abuse by my husband. And he has controlled and limited my contact with my daughters. I am still fighting to regain custody of them. What helped me keep fighting during those twelve years of domestic violence? I discovered personal development.

In April 2011, I took a seminar in Lyon, France, called Business Passion with Roger Lannoy and Lionel Donneley, two mentors who have done Tony Robbins's Mastery University. With the help of a mind map, I found one of my passions: the human condition, meaning how we operate, our personal development. At first, I couldn't believe it. It was too big a concept for me, and I couldn't imagine how to transform it into a business. But, step by step, I started to accept it, because I saw that everything I did had the goal of helping other people. Two years later, I created a nonprofit association to help thousands of people live their passions with the autonomy to manage their businesses on their own.

In November 2014, I asked the universe which tool I should use to help my clients discover their passions. And, of course, the answer came: I received an email about the Passion Test from Positive Jessica, or Jessica Pereira, the first French-speaking master trainer. I immediately submitted my candidacy to participate in the facilitator certification in Paris in February 2015.

Unfortunately, I was in a very complicated situation just when I found out how I could help my clients. I had been homeless since July, as I had sold my house to pay my debts. I was in a collective settlement of my debt, and the mediator wouldn't give me a cent until the judge made his decision. I couldn't find a house because I had no payroll records (I had a pension from the Belgian government since November 2010, after which I was self-employed). So I asked Jessica to wait a bit for the payment for the training so that I could find a solution.

I found a house to rent on December 5. On February 9, I finally recouped some of my financial losses, not from the mediator of the collective settlement but from the notary, after the death of my father in May 2014. I could pay for the training in Paris! It was a real opportunity that I could go. I quickly reserved the train and hotel and arranged to share a room with another participant.

This training was a revelation for me and showed me what was really important—I discovered my passions. My top five passions remain almost the same to this day:

1. To be a worldwide Passion Test facilitator and Master Trainer.
2. To have a fulfilling and complementary relationship.
3. To have a good relationship and connection with my girls.
4. To help thousands of people live their passions.
5. To have total abundance.

I can tell from the fulfillment of my markers that everything I asked for is now coming into my life in a very clear way.

In March 2015, I went to Australia for the Passion Test for Business, in English. In October 2015, I attended the annual reunion in San Diego, and I linked up with the Passion Test for Kids and Teens. This one is my favorite, because I would like to continue helping children with autism, Asperger's syndrome, and high potential find meaning in their lives. In Belgium, the school system is not adapted for them.

In November 2015, I was an assistant at the second Passion Test facilitator certification in Paris. I did the Passion Test again there and saw that my eighth passion was to have exceptional moments with my Passion Test family. And I learned that my first business passion was to travel all over the world with the Passion

Test family. The next month, Janet proposed that I participate in the upcoming Advanced Master Training in Copenhagen. I had exceptional moments there with members of the Passion Test family from eight different nationalities. We had a terrific time together; once more, the universe answered my wishes.

In February 2016, I participated in the Master Training for the Passion Test for Kids and Teens. I am so excited to help children, teenagers, and young people around the French-speaking world so that they can discover their passions—and so that their parents can, too.

I also have a mission to complete in the French-speaking African countries that have survived war. I'm in contact with the young people of these countries, and they have asked me to help them and are talking with their parents about me. I know they anxiously await my arrival. What encourages me to help the young people and their parents in African countries is a sentence from my childhood: "Give a man a fish and you will feed him for a day; teach a man to fish and you feed him for a lifetime." My mission is to teach them to fish in their own country so that they can rebuild it themselves and not believe that Europe is a paradise. I want to help them fish from their passions and develop qualities and natural talents they already have inside them.

For me, the most important Passion Test principle is the Passion Test formula for creating anything you want in your life: Intention, Attention, No Tension. This formula—with my belief that if you want, you can do anything—is the evidence that I can have, be, or do anything I want in my life. I just have to put my attention on a clear intention, and then let go and follow the flow.

Veronique Scheldeman is a national director of the Passion Test and the Passion Test for Kids and Teens. In the nineties, she was a tax inspector for corporations, and then a labor inspector. In 2010, she left her career as a controller with the Belgian government to return to her main purpose in life: helping others. She has perfected various methods of personal development, such as PEAT (Primordial Energy Activation and Transcendence) and the Listen to Your Body school of Lise Bourbeau. She helps people get started in business by living their passions through the Passion Test and helps people unlock their emotions and their potential with the work of Lise Bourbeau. To see what Veronique is working on, send her an email at Veronique@ thepassiontest.com, or visit her website at businesspassionenfants.com. This is a French website, but you can email her in English.

Chapter 10

THE PASSION TEST SECRET— IT'S NO SECRET AT ALL

Patty Blakesley

There are hundreds of suggestions for how to change your life or live your best life. How do you sort through them all? The first time I did the Passion Test, I gained exquisite clarity and appreciation for everything in my life. When I came to see that my life uniquely qualified me to be me, I was free from searching. I was buoyant. Suddenly, a truer sense of purpose and freedom empowered me. I was onstage, and I stood in the spotlight. I could do what I knew in my heart felt right, and quickly my priorities shifted.

90

At that point in my life, I was in my sixties, and I was the main caregiver for my octogenarian mother. Seven years earlier, I had semi-retired and moved from my longtime home on Martha's Vineyard to my birth state of Wisconsin. My mother, who had settled near me when she retired from her job twenty years earlier, returned as well. An island in the Atlantic was a long way from where most of our family lived.

Soon after I moved, I studied to be a tax preparer and a real estate agent. I kept myself busy working part-time at each of these jobs. I continued my practice of karate. I wrote and read. I traveled as much as I could. Everything was just regular and ordinary. I did not realize how limited my life had become until I immersed myself in the Passion Test.

The first step is to imagine your life as ideal without being limited by time or money. My memory bank spilled open. I knew I loved karate and my friends, but I rarely chose in favor of me. I had long ago given up one of my first loves: horses. And although I loved writing, I hardly had time to do any. What else had I denied myself during my topsy-turvy life?

My choice as a younger woman to live on Martha's Vineyard restricted my work options. Martha's Vineyard is amazing in its physical beauty, but it is an expensive resort that is also one of the poorest counties in the state. A day at the beach was a rarity for me. I did so many different jobs that I lost count. I worked for nonprofits, governments, and private businesses. Mortgage loan officer, a children's librarian assistant, a household hazardous waste technician, a secretary, a bookkeeper—and the list goes on. I struggled to earn enough to support my only son and myself after my first divorce, and, sadly, after my second.

Shortly after moving to Martha's Vineyard, I thought about horseback riding, as I'd ridden as a child. But I never did. My best friend since before first grade, Leslie, lived in western Colorado. Her Christmas cards came with snowy vistas and galloping horses. Over the years, she'd asked me to visit her. But I never did. I hadn't ridden for decades, because I said I would never pay a horse more an hour than I earned. What a limiting belief I created to keep me from one of my passions!

Here are my original passions. When my life is ideal,

1. I am enjoying the practice of karate with my friends,
2. I am writing with the intention to create love in the world,
3. I am having fun with horses and other animals,
4. I am living in a spiritual partnership with my beloved, and
5. I am connecting with friends and family.

"Whenever you're given a decision, a choice, or an opportunity, choose in favor of your passions." This is the Passion Test secret. For me the secret is like a beam from a lighthouse. Follow it and you will avoid danger. You will find a safe harbor. You will find joy.

Memories of the joy I experienced riding my horse when I was a troubled teenager invaded my thoughts, even my dreams. I heard my horse, Honeycomb, neighing. I could practically smell the barn. The Passion Test helped me remember what I loved to do.

After taking the Passion Test, I remembered that one of my real estate clients told me her daughter took lessons at a nearby farm where the horses were ridden without a bit. I always hated putting that cold hunk of metal in my horse's mouth, futilely attempting to warm it with my icy hands in winter, and I was excited to treat horses with more care. I called up Jody Halladay at 16 Acres Equine Educational Complex and started taking lessons in natural horsemanship. This is a horse training system based on understanding a horse's nature and behavior, and developing a relationship with it. To a horse lover, a connection with a warm and loving animal is a spiritual experience. A horse treated with care and consideration is a joy to ride, to groom, or to own.

Six months after taking the Passion Test, Leslie invited me to visit her again. In early October, the San Juan mountain range near her home was ablaze with yellow aspen trees. A week before I arrived, an early snowstorm had frosted the mountains. The views stunned me. Although I hadn't gained total confidence in the saddle yet, I was delighted to be out in the wilderness with my oldest friend, riding trails in the Rockies with her horses. Seeing cattle driven down from their summer range, watching photographers from all over the country hike miles for rare shots of snow and yellow aspens, I felt one of my passions come alive.

My lessons in natural horsemanship continue, and I look forward to more great rides. I've brought my youngest great-niece, Chloe, out to Jody's farm, and she started lessons at age six. Driving to and from the barn, Chloe and I play road games and talk. I love it. Connecting with family and friends is another one of my passions, and this shared experience is something I never could have imagined before I started following the Passion Test secret.

Plus, I've begun volunteering with a nonprofit organization that rescues horses, Namaste Equine Rescue. In the summer of 2015, the American Quarter Horse Association sponsored a Time to Ride Challenge. We participated by introducing horses to more than ten thousand people at local fairs and community events in southeastern Wisconsin. Scores of volunteers contributed many hours, but the time spent was worth it when young kids felt a horse or stroked its neck. My favorite participant was an elderly woman who confided that she had wanted to touch a horse her entire life. She was bent over as she walked toward our spotted pony and cautiously lifted her hand to stroke its soft coat. Her face beamed with a smile I'll never forget.

I could go on about my love of horses, and friends and family, because I feel so connected with these passions. But I want to touch on my passion for writing.

Since I was a kid, I have loved words and writing. Over the years, I've taken numerous courses from some kind and generous teachers. In a lot of my jobs, I found opportunities to write articles for newsletters, and I always wrote plenty of letters to clients. As a volunteer with various environmental and community organizations, I wrote letters to the editors of papers and press releases galore. I was even paid to write a weekly column for a local paper on one of my favorite topics: the environment. I loved doing it, but I stopped because I felt that my pay did not justify the time it took. Once again, I let money turn me away from what I loved.

After certifying to be a Passion Test facilitator, I received an email about a writing course. I don't remember ever seeing one before. I opened it without hesitation. I saw it as an opportunity and signed up without question, even though it cost money and I would have to drive a considerable distance during the winter months. Driving in a snowstorm is not my idea of fun, but I drove to every class. Judy Bridges, author of *Shut Up & Write!*, is a master teacher, and I have never regretted my decision.

One of my dilemmas about writing was always what to focus on, since I like to write almost everything, including poems, articles, short stories, and memoirs. Judy suggested that I pick the project that most excited me. When my life is ideal, I'm writing with the intention to increase love in the world. The Passion Test helped me see that I have a choice to reflect my values when I write.

I'm now writing a fantasy novel for teenagers. The main conflict between the tyrannical leadership of the country and the dragons it enslaved is resolved without war and violence. If we keep giving kids the same tales of good versus evil resolved through war, will we ever build a better world based on love? Gary Zukav, author and respected transformational leader, talks about the need to promote peace, harmony, sharing, and reverence for life. I believe strongly in these values and applied them to my story. I asked myself these questions: Does killing an ogre promote reverence for life? Wouldn't his mother weep at his grave? Whether or not my story gets published, I'm confident that I'm writing what is true to my heart.

The Passion Test also includes the concept of markers. Markers are evidence that you're living your passion, or signs that you're well on your way. After I determined my top five passions, I developed three to five markers for each one. The invitation to visit my friend in Colorado was a marker. Being given a horse is another marker for me. That email about the writing course was not a marker I had envisioned, but it could have been. And being published is another marker. I read my most recent poems to one of my friends and experienced another marker when she told me I had a book.

Making markers is a fun part of the process of imagining an ideal life. Many of the passions I did not choose for my top five became markers. For example, one of my passions was that when my life is ideal, I am living a joyful life. Believe me, when I am working with kids who are learning karate, I am enjoying my life. And feeding my lesson horse peppermints is a moment of pure joy.

"Whenever you're given a decision, a choice or an opportunity, choose in favor of your passions." Although the Passion Test secret never changes, the process is not static. My passion of enjoying karate with my friends has evolved to be when my life is ideal, my friends and I are enjoying a profitable income from teaching karate. One of our markers is a wildly successful dojo, or training facility. I meet regularly with my karate family in Illinois to make this happen. Are we there yet? No, but we're on our way.

The Passion Test exemplifies the power of an undeniable belief that change can happen. As a Passion Test facilitator, I've worked with friends, family, and total strangers. Those who've come with an open mind and a belief in change have found the most success. I had to chuckle at myself when I worked with my massage therapist to reorder her passions, because within a few weeks, she put her business up for sale. Now she lives in Florida—and I had to find a new massage therapist.

If I had a tip for anyone interested in the Passion Test, it would be to trust the process. Harvard Business School professor emerita Rosabeth Moss Kanter wrote a book entitled *Confidence: How Winning and Losing Streaks Begin and End.* She explains that confidence is the only thing that can really turn things around. As she said in an article in *Realtor* magazine in 2009, "Confidence is what motivates you to put in resources because you expect you'll get a positive return. Once success starts, it becomes easier to keep investing because confidence is high."

This describes my experience with the Passion Test. I expected a positive outcome, and I've had success. Now I expect more positive outcomes, and I will invest more time and effort in my passions. I trust the process. I am inspired to continue to develop my abilities and discover my gifts. I hope you'll be as well. Trust that you're always on the right path: your path. There may be unexpected twists and turns, but they're there for a reason.

The Passion Test has given me a direction and a belief that whatever I focus on can be mine. I sometimes feel as if I'm a squirmy caterpillar metamorphosing. I'm not saying that everything in the process is easy. There are struggles and choices. I'm reminded that without the struggle to break out of its cocoon, the luna moth will wither and die. I follow the Passion Test secret, and that's really no secret at all. I recommend you do, too. I predict you'll be amazed at what shows up in your life.

Patty Blakesley is a resident of the world but lives in the heartland of North America. Her interests include karate, horses, birds, bicycling, and writing. She enjoys living moment to moment and finds each one fascinating. She earned her third-degree black belt in 2013 with the World Shorin-Ryu Federation and is an assistant instructor at the Goho Seishin dojo in Lake Villa, Illinois (www. gohoseishin.com). Check out her blog at www.pattyblakesley.com and receive her free ebook, Black Belt Tips for Living Fully. *Patty and her Living Fully team offer coaching, business consulting, empowerment workshops, and inspirational talks. Patty's email is patty.blakesley@ gmail.com, and she promises to answer every one.*

Chapter 11

ANYTHING IS POSSIBLE
WITH CLARITY

Susanne Knudsen

I first met Janet Bray Attwood around November 2014 at a Steinar Ditlefsen seminar where she was a guest speaker. I had no idea who Janet was, so from day one, I was wondering, *who is she, and what can she help me with?* The more I heard Janet talk about how the Passion Test came to life, and what difference it made in her life, the more curious I got about how I could take the Passions Test, because that was not on the program. Day two had an interesting start because there were a lot of complaints about the program and one speaker did not come as she was supposed to. I was in luck because Steinar chose Janet to give us the Passion Test in her place. I was so happy in that moment, almost jumping up and down in my seat, like a child at Christmas, even though I had no idea what to expect.

My first Passion Test showed me some of the things I already knew deep down but had a hard time explaining. I had tried to live a life on other people's terms, and it had resulted in stress and depression. It took me only two minutes to decide to take the Passion Test facilitator course. I just knew that the Passion Test could give me the missing clarity that I needed to create exactly the life that I wanted for myself.

At that time, I was running two companies and had created a life where I had the financial freedom to make the decisions that were right for me. My biggest challenge was the fact that I had been ill for thirty-five years, an illness that had shown up in many different ways throughout my life. Six months into my three years of being self-employed, leading up to my meeting with Janet, I broke my collarbone, and I didn't sleep for a year. After that, I became very ill and was almost unable to run my companies. Later, it turned out food allergies were the cause of my illness.

In February 2015, I was feeling overwhelmed in many areas of my life, so when I took the Passion Test for the second time, I realized that of course I could not get healthy as long as I let my illness be the reason for me to not live my passions to the fullest. So I plunged in and decided to enroll in the advanced program Janet offered to help Passion Test facilitators grow their businesses. This six-month course gave me access to a lot of material and a mentor in the U.S. I knew I stood at a crossroads, so two weeks later, I booked a trip to the USA to visit my aunt, and in the fourteen days I was there, I read through all the material for the advanced program. This wasn't a light read, since Janet has truly provided a vast amount of useful content.

The more I read the material, the more I realized it was knowledge I had already accumulated in my sixteen years of work. It was incredibly valuable for me to read what Chris and Janet had written, because I finally had a structure for the wisdom I already possessed but had taken for granted, or had simply forgotten to implement in my life. When I came home to Denmark, I had my first session with my mentor, Beth. We went through my passions and adjusted them. With Beth's help, my passions were as follows:

1. I have the freedom to follow my heart and dreams.
2. I make a transformational difference for others that changes their lives.
3. I travel the world.
4. I enjoy healthy and loving relationships with inspiring people who share my passions.
5. I experience a complete family life with a husband and kids in harmony and support.

Once I had my passions and the markers down, I immediately started making all my decisions with my passions in mind. To this day I don't say yes to anything unless I can see it bringing me closer to living my passions. In addition, I made a structured plan for how I could create a life in which I would actually be able to live my passions fully. This plan led to the creation of another company, Din Passion, based in Denmark, where I help others find their passions and create businesses where they live their passions.

At that point, something interesting happened concerning my illness. This was my marker for my number one passion: I'm 100 percent healthy and well and happy every day, and people around me notice and congratulate me.

What happened was the complete opposite. I got more and more sick. After talking about it for a while, Beth and I realized that of course I was going to get more sick, because I had no control over my illness, and that meant that I had no idea which foods made me sick.

I kept on fighting, even though I was having a very hard time. The allergies had attacked my vocal cords, and I developed new symptoms every day for six weeks. But fate had arranged for me to meet a woman named Mette who showed me how I could use kinesiology to test my food before eating it. Once I knew what foods made me sick, it was easy to avoid them.

In one week, I had sorted out all of the foods that were not good for me. After that, Janet helped me get in contact with some people in the U.S. who had forty years of experience with my illness—"high gluten sensitivity." This led to another course, this time as a gluten practitioner. The funny thing about all of this was that I found a new passion for helping people get healthy, which led me to create a new company that sells dietary supplements that re-create balance in your omega-3 and omega-6 fatty acids and thereby eliminate inflammation. I found out during the course that this was crucial for people with my illness. With my new knowledge, I can easily say that I've extended my lifespan by an extra ten to twenty years.

With the help of the Passion Test, Janet, and my mentor, I was able to get full control over my illness within four months, and I now know that it is only a matter of time before I can enjoy all foods again.

Eight months after I took the Passion Test the second time, I had created the life I wanted for myself. I'd started three new companies and have another on the way. One of my companies already broke 100,000 krone (about US$15,000) in sales in one month.

I now live two of my passions fully:

1. I have the freedom to follow my heart and dreams, and
2. I travel the world.

The one passion that has been really tricky for me is number five: I experience a complete family life with a husband and kids in harmony and support. When I took the Passion Test for the second time, this was a completely new passion for me, and the woman who took me through the test looked at me and said, "That one surprised you, didn't it?" Yes, I must say it really did.

My relationship with my parents complicated my ability to find a husband and build a family. I've had a lot of conflict with my parents because of personal difficulties, patterns, and convictions that had built up over my thirty-five years, but I knew it was me who had to change, because they were merely a reflection of the demons I struggled with.

After that shift came the realization that my family was my passion number five the first time I took the test. How could I push them away when they meant so much to me? I went to see my parents the weekend after I took the Passion Test, to take them through the test. First, it gave them an understanding of what the Passion Test was, since I had been talking so much about it, and second, it gave me a completely different understanding of my parents. When I saw their top five passions, and we could talk about why they were as they were, it really brought us closer. Today, I have a great relationship with my mother and father, and I managed to break nothing less than four major patterns, one of which went back several generations on my father's side of the family.

My relationship with my parents was not the only difficulty I had with this passion. At the time, I doubted whether I truly wanted a husband and kids. After spending the last thirty-five years being ill and building my career, I had pretty much shut down anything to do with men. As time went by after solving my problems with my parents, I fell back into old patterns. This meant that I put all my energy and focus on fulfilling my other passions, all but number five.

One day, one of my business partners said, "Susanne, you can't keep challenging me on my love life, if you don't do anything about your own." I knew deep down she was right, because Janet had taught us the formula of Intention, Attention, No Tension. What you put your attention on and take action on grows stronger in your life as long as you stay open to new possibilities appearing.

I had manifested all of the other things in my life, but what kept me from taking action on passion number five was passion number one. I seriously doubted my ability to create exactly the life I wanted and still have the freedom to follow my heart and dreams.

I had been dating for the previous three years, with no serious relationship. With my knowledge of the Passion Test and the law of attraction, I started writing lists of what I liked and did not like about all of the men I met. After that, I turned the things I disliked around and put only positive qualities all on one list. Then I burned up the negative list so that I could stop attracting the bad things and be completely clear on what I did want in my life. On top of that, I started being grateful for all of the men in my everyday life. I started noticing all of the positive things they did for the people around them and for themselves.

Slowly but steadily, the list of things that deep down meant something to me in relationships grew longer. The day my business partner took my phone to sign me up for Tinder, my immediate thought was *No thanks*, but after thinking about it for a couple of hours, I got curious and thought, *Maybe this is exactly the challenge I need*. I started swiping left and right, and the first match showed up pretty quickly. We went on a date and had really good chemistry, and I thought, *Oh wow, it's crazy to meet someone who matches me and my passions so well and so quickly*. So when he asked me if I wanted to go on a vacation with him, I immediately said yes, because I knew that if I wanted to succeed on my passion number five, I would have to do something completely out of character.

I started living my life in opposites, which meant that when I needed to make a decision, I chose the opposite of what I would normally do. The vacation went well, but we both soon realized that he had great resistance to the way I lived my life, and I was confronted by my own beliefs and old patterns. After a week on vacation with him, I had learned a whole lot about myself, because every time a conflict arose or there was something I didn't understand, I looked within and asked myself to find the answers to what it was all about.

One week after getting home, I woke up in the middle of the night and it was clear to me: I was not supposed to change myself to be with a man; I am worth loving just the way I am. In that moment, I broke three major patterns all at once: I did not think I was good enough; I was finding ways to get the guy to love me, without being true to myself; and I was always pleasing a guy so that he would be with me. Already the next day I could see evidence of the shift that had happened in me. I kept working on the lists of what I liked and disliked about the men I met in my day-to-day life to become more aware of and more clear about what kind of man I wanted to attract.

The big change happened when I talked to my mentor and told her that I was actually completely fine whether I found a man or not, because either way, I had created a pretty amazing life for myself over the last eight months. I'd been living my passions fully and doing whatever I wanted. So, I deleted the contacts on my Tinder profile and let go of the men I'd attracted on my journey so far.

A few days later, I was messing around on my phone because I was bored, and I got curious and checked in on Tinder. I had forty-four matches in four hours, one of whom was an incredibly nice man. Meeting him and seeing how much he supported me and how I felt with him made me realize how much I wanted a family and children.

When I took the Passion Test, my experience with this wonderful man raised passion number five to passion number two. I've learned that it's very important to take the Passion Test every six months, because your passions can change or be fulfilled, which means you can start working on your passion numbers six and seven. The more you learn about and live your passions, the more clarity you get so that you can make the right choices. I've learned in my journey with the Passion Test that anything is possible.

Susanne Knudsen is a facilitator of healthy choices. With passion, motivation, and energy, she helps people and businesses achieve lifelong change, enabling them to live their lives and create businesses that match their wishes and passions. She helps people achieve a healthy lifestyle, business, relationships, body, thoughts, and stories by means of her specialty in the complete person. She applies a holistic approach, as you cannot realize a great life and be successful if there is an imbalance between your five elements: Faith, Foundation, Economy, Relationships, and Health. She uses them every day in her professional life as an entrepreneur with five companies and in her personal life. Find Susanne online at www.susanneknudsen.com.

Chapter 12

FROM ZERO TO HERO:
A LOST SOUL TRANSFORMS
INTO AN ENERGY HEALER

Jens-Simon Ulvoy

"The only thing I care about is awakening."
—Kiara Windrider

*W*hen I was a small boy, I was totally innocent, living on a small island surrounded by ocean and other islands on all sides. There was only my family around and no friends nearby to play games with in the evening. It was an incredible situation, when I think back on it. I have met many people from nearly all corners of the world, but I have yet to meet anyone with that extremely rural background. Even in Norway, my family was exceptional in its isolation and loneliness.

When I was a few years older, around fifteen or sixteen, I had the distinct feeling that I wanted to do good work for other people. I wanted to be a good person, who didn't harm others but helped them instead. That feeling followed me through my teens and later, even when I was not taking any serious action to help others.

In May 2014, I had been searching for something for an extended period of time, reading, wondering about the big questions. I was always looking for something new, the missing bit of information that could fall into place and move my life into an upswing. The seeker in me was always on the lookout for a turning point.

I was going to attend the Golden Life Program (GLP) seminar weekend in Tokyo on the invitation of my wife, Kaori. The list of speakers contained names that I had hardly heard about, but it felt right to attend and I was looking forward to it with excitement. This was going to be another thrilling seminar in a long chain of seminars I had attended—and self-help books I had read—over many years.

I was introduced to the Passion Test by Janet Attwood on the first morning of the seminar. And what an experience it was! All of the presenters were world-class in their own ways, but in front of the audience of more than seven hundred, Janet stood out in particular, with an amazing energy, smile, and likeable attitude. Her presence wowed me and triggered the feeling of wanting to be someone like that, speaking effortlessly in front of a large audience. I was totally taken by surprise by her energy and how natural her performance was.

I took the Passion Test that morning, and my top five passions were:

1. Living an inspired life, helping other people
2. Exercising every day in top physical form
3. Enjoying a wonderful relationship with my wife
4. Living life as a public speaker
5. Having time and financial freedom

I felt relief and the feeling that things were falling into place, that everything on my list was natural and meant to be, like a traditional homecoming when your family smiles and welcomes you back. At the same time, I was surprised, because my current way of life and my background, and that of most of my family and friends, was a regular, typical lifestyle. But then I discovered some passions that were so different from the reality that I was used to living for most of my life.

After discovering my number one passion, to live an inspired life helping others, I realized I had a deep desire, born out of love, to heal my father. Sometimes I had this dark thought that my family, particularly my father, was doomed. He suffered a stroke before I was born and never fully recovered. He started forgetting things when I was around ten years old and some years later developed Alzheimer's disease, at which point he totally lost control of his life and forgot his family and surroundings. This was before the Internet and the ability to search quickly for everything. I had absolutely no idea what his condition was, and neither did anyone else in my family. The act of helping others and being inspired, like healing my father, is a self-healing process, which is another reason why I feel a strong need to help others.

During that first day of the seminar, when the possibility was offered to take a course that would qualify me to facilitate others taking the Passion Test, I found myself thinking for two long seconds. Before lunch, I had decided to follow at least two of my newly discovered passions and take the course for Passion Test facilitators coming up only two months later.

The first really lasting change in my life came very quickly after taking the Passion Test for the first time and returning home from that seminar.

Drinking alcohol is a very deep part of Western culture, and I was very embedded in that culture. I used to tell my wife I would stop drinking in "around two to three years." That promise typically happened the morning after a night of heavy drinking with friends, when I was shrouded in a heavy hangover cloud that seemed to grow darker after each bout. This became a pattern, occurring perhaps two or three times a year.

On the Monday after taking the Passion Test, I suddenly got the feeling that alcohol and drinking no longer interested me. It was like discovering a new reality, and I was incredibly surprised by this. I thought of myself as a normal person who "enjoyed" drinking, but then there I sat by myself over lunch and, out of the blue, had the feeling that drinking wasn't for me anymore. My life and many friends revolved around meetings that included drinking that I no longer found satisfying. I can only describe the reason why I stopped casual drinking as a feeling from deep inside my heart. I had a totally new experience when I focused my attention on what I truly wanted. And that experience has followed me since I got clarity from taking the Passion Test that first time.

After a couple of months of waiting and raised expectations, I attended the Passion Test facilitator course. This four-day course truly changed the way I looked at life and myself. I learned about the technicalities of organizing a three-hour workshop and, more important, a variety of techniques for opening my heart to other people.

By far the biggest change that happened to me during the course was on the closing of the third day. We formed a big circle around the room and everyone said one word that summed up the day for them, their feeling in that moment. Looking around the room at all the people around me, I could see each individual and their uniqueness. It was as if I saw the raw potential in each person and that each and every one had a special talent. It was a very strong emotional moment. I thought about Buddha's words that each one of us has the potential for enlightenment, and in that small fraction of a second, I felt a divine power was showing me the truth of that statement. It was a profound and lasting experience that I think about very often.

During the facilitator course, I took the Passion Test again, and I found that my top five passions had changed only slightly since the first time. I realized again, *Wow, this is what I really want to do,* and I asked myself, *Is this really who you are?* The Passion Test formula of Intention, Attention, No Tension clarified for me the necessity of knowing what you want before trying to achieve it.

Meeting the Passion Test family also reminded me to have curiosity about life and other people. When I was a child, attending university, living abroad, and traveling internationally were foreign concepts and totally outside of my world. But after several vocational jobs and military service, I felt dissatisfied with my life and finally decided to move into academia. One of my best decisions was to go to university—first in Norway and then in the U.K. Studying opened my eyes and mind thoroughly to the wider world. And through the Passion Test, I have made many international friendships that have enriched my life and opened my perspective.

For example, I learned that I'm overly sensitive to personal criticism. I really, really dislike when someone points out a fault, flaw, mistake, or something I did or did not do. This quality applies to my job, my hobbies, or whatever I have made a commitment to. I feel hot, my head spins, and there is an uncomfortable feeling in my stomach. I cannot understand why I react like this. It seems I have always had this feeling. I thought it would disappear when I became an adult, but it didn't. I have discovered some tricks to reduce or avoid this feeling, either by bolstering my self-confidence, which happened after I discovered the Passion Test, or by simply thinking that I don't need this situation, place, or person in my life anymore. That's a liberating thought.

I discovered another freeing technique when I learned about Nature's Guidance System of contraction and expansion, how to notice the difference between the two, and that all feelings are right in every moment. Understanding how to use this principle was an enormous awakening for me—there's nothing wrong with feeling down or gloomy. When I was first presented with so many clear examples of this way of thinking during the Passion Test facilitator's course and during the master training, I realized we are all responsible for our own thoughts and feelings, and for how we react to other people's words about us.

My journey continued when my wife and I met up with other Passion Test facilitators at the Passion Test reunion that happens every autumn in San Diego. We had such a wonderful time meeting people from a variety of countries. The reunion weekend was full of having fun, forming new relationships, and experiencing firsthand how many different people have been transformed through the Passion Test and are now sharing it with others. I learned something from everyone. I met healers and was really impressed and influenced by the thoughts about planetary healing or awakening of Kiara Windrider, for example. After the Passion Test reunion, my network of positive-minded people was greatly expanded.

Some of the people I kept in touch with after the reunion are living a lifestyle of traveling from their home base to many faraway places and offering healing workshops. We got well acquainted and I invited them to Tokyo to organize a full-day energy workshop. We advertised it with an attractive flyer in both English and Japanese, and collected a group of people who were interested in learning this new technique for energizing themselves as speakers or presenters. I felt an immense gratitude for and sense of purpose by experiencing an energetic healing firsthand. I also participated in the workshop and, after going through the instruction, could practice energetic healing myself. The immediate and most appealing result was a tickling sensation in the palms of my hands, and I can reproduce that feeling each and every time I practice this healing technique.

After the workshop, everyone gathered around, sharing smiles, positive feelings, and well-being in each other's company; offering words of encouragement; and spreading an atmosphere of inner joy. That was a priceless moment in my life, totally meaningful as the only right place for me to be and thing for me to do. This is the true meaning of living a passionate life, I realized, and it unfolded in front of my eyes effortlessly and naturally. It was the feeling of being in the flow, without having to do anything out of stress.

I have experienced the Passion Test as a self-healing process, empowered and amplified by the formula of Intention, Attention, No Tension, in which the positive life force reigns and the belief in the universe as a superb organizing principle unfolds. If I can live according to the Passion Test principles, you can, too. Opening my heart and feeling inner peace, gratitude, and joy for the real things in life are my everlasting gifts from discovering the Passion Test.

Jens-Simon Ulvoy comes from rural Northern Norway, and studied and worked in London and Oslo before obtaining long-term residency in Tokyo. His journey has been filled with a wealth of experiences living and adapting to another culture while enjoying an international multicultural working environment. After Jens discovered his passion for living an inspired life helping others, he immediately decided to follow this path. Jens has participated in

the Passion Test certification, Master Trainer, and Passion Test for Business programs. Interests such as cooking, travel, transcendental meditation, snowboarding, hiking, exercising, and sailing are even more fun with passion.

Chapter 13

BE POSITIVE AND YOU'LL BE POWERFUL!

Elayna Fernández, the Positive MOM

$\mathcal{J}$ was tired, but I couldn't sleep. Even though it was two o'clock in the morning, I decided to get up. When I turned on the lights, I realized my husband, Eric, wasn't home yet. Something was wrong!

Suddenly, the 125-square-foot room where we lived felt as big as an ocean. *Where is he?* I wondered as doubt and fear filled my mind. I had no phone or computer to contact him. Maybe he was stuck at work, but in the pit of my stomach, I knew differently.

Frantic, I ran outside in my pajamas and scanned the street for his car. It wasn't there. Now in a panic, I returned to our room and realized Eric's clothes were gone!

Then I saw the letter—it had been right there the whole time. I read the words as my heart pounded in my chest. *By the time you read this, you will probably realize I've left and won't be coming back,* the letter read.

I wanted to scream, but I didn't have the strength. I fell to my knees and curled into the fetal position on the cold floor. Pressing my stomach, I sensed an unfamiliar emptiness that spread like cancer and hurt like no other pain I'd ever felt before.

Someone tell me this is only a nightmare! I begged. *Tell me I'll wake up and everything will be fine...*

A few days earlier, we'd arrived in Florida after a week-long cross-country drive from Southern California to close on a new home and "live happily ever after." My fairy tale had vanished.

The flashbacks began playing in my head. Having grown up in extreme poverty in the Dominican Republic, and enduring trauma from my parents' divorce and the unhealthy dynamics that come from an impulsive and abusive mother, I had vowed to never get married or have children, and to focus only on my personal development, success, and career.

I became an entrepreneur at age seven, finished high school as a star student at age fifteen, and enrolled in English as a second language classes, eventually teaching at the same center where I'd been taught—all before my sixteenth birthday. When it was time to go to college, I overcame every challenge to pursue what I wanted. I did not let anything discourage me or anyone derail me. I was unstoppable.

I was able to transfer to a private university, where my proficiency in English and outstanding grades earned me entry into the Work and Travel program and a J-1 visa to the United

States in 1999. That summer in Michigan, along with so many other amazing experiences, I met Eric, and we began our long-distance relationship.

Meeting him changed my mind about marriage and children. But the thought of moving to the United States never crossed my mind. As a matter of fact, as soon as I went back to the Dominican Republic, I bought a condo and surrounded myself with beautiful furnishings as I enjoyed life in my country.

I had it all figured out. Eric would transfer to the U.S. embassy, I would continue my work as chief operating officer at the Technology Park, I would get my marketing degree, and my family could help with the children.

Eric and I did marry in the Dominican Republic, but the transfer never happened, and I ended up leaving the life of my dreams in order "to make my marriage work." I went from being happily surrounded by loving and supportive friends and family, and enjoying a successful career, to being "barefoot and pregnant in the kitchen."

As I knelt on the floor, these memories haunted me, and I berated myself. *How could I have been so foolish, and how did I get so derailed from my deepest purpose? What happened to the bold, confident, driven, joyful woman I'd once been?* I desperately wanted to be that confident woman again, to drag her out of the deepest parts of my being. But was she gone forever?

I felt pathetic, knowing I'd been living a lie, forgetting who I once was, and putting aside my own desires and sense of self. With a deep sense of guilt, regret, and overwhelming fear, I blamed myself for becoming so vulnerable, for every mistake I had made, and for being tangled in this downward spiral. Divorce meant failure... my failure. I couldn't believe my marriage was over after only three years! At the age of twenty-eight, I decided once more that marriage was not for me.

Alone, ashamed, and without a penny to my name, stuck in this one-room "efficiency" rental without a kitchen, I didn't have a job or a car. I didn't even know how to drive! I thought it was a tasteless joke that Eric had left the girls' car seats behind. I was so angry that I'd ever believed in and loved him.

In the midst of my self-pity, self-doubt, and self-defeat, I took a long, deep breath and suddenly felt a moment of inspiration to do three things that completely changed my experience:

1. **I looked UP.** I saw my little angel girls peacefully asleep, and my anger and desperation melted away. I realized I hadn't lost it all. I hugged them carefully so that they wouldn't wake up and thanked God they were safe and in my life. My breath seemed to slow as I held them tight, knowing they were worth all the pain, anxiety, and drama I'd endured in my dysfunctional, unfulfilling, and abusive marriage that was now over.

The most meaningful moments in life teach us that it is not *what* we have that matters but *who* we have. And I had the BEST part, my most cherished treasures.

My lesson from this was that when we start focusing on gratitude and love instead of scarcity and fear, we open up to greater possibilities, to see ourselves as God sees us and the destiny He has for each of us.

My babies didn't have a clue that their lives were changed forever. As I sighed in relief, I decided they didn't have to know— at least not yet.

2. **I asked, What if?** *What if I could have it all?* What if I could turn it all around and offer my daughters a life of JOY? What if they could grow to have BALANCE and experience SUCCESS? I started to visualize their entrepreneurial journeys, their joyful play, even their weddings! *Is that possible for a single mom?* I thought of Roberto Benigni's Academy Award–winning performance in *Life Is Beautiful* and smiled, remembering how a parent can make the most dreadful horrors seem like the most fun games to an innocent child. *I can do that*, I thought, and immediately a glimmer of hope rose within me. In the middle of my dark agony, I found comfort in a vision of love.

3. **I released the HOW.** Now that I was clear about my ideal life, I thought the action plan would come easily, but having lived in confinement as a housemaid to my ex-husband for the past few years did not exactly prepare me to face this situation. I really didn't have the background, knowledge, or support to come up with any next steps. I was just learning how to be a mom, and I had never been a *single* mom, in a new town, in a country that didn't feel like home.

"How?" can be a disempowering question, because it reveals the gap between where we are and where we want to be. I didn't want to live my life depressed, defeated, and depleted... I wanted to reset my life, reinvent myself, and reap the rewards. And that's when I made the list. It wasn't a to-do list... it was a to-BE list. It was a list of who I needed to be to live an empowered life. I decided that in order to be powerful, I had to take responsibility for my life and focus on the positive, like I had done just a few seconds before. I realized I had the power to create my life... anytime.

The days that followed were difficult. I felt stuck in the United States because I couldn't leave until I proved myself worthy of being granted legal custody of my daughters. People said, "It will all get better in time," but I soon realized time is no healer. I fought frequently with feelings of inadequacy and low self-worth. The feeling of failure crept in more often than I care to admit. I sought consolation in infrequent telephone conversations with my family and friends in my homeland, and in my prayers. I prayed fervently for miracles, and lo and behold, they began to manifest.

My brother sent me his life savings so that I could rent a small place in Naples, Florida, where an old friend worked as an apartment manager. Learning how to drive was terrifying because it brought back traumatic memories. But I was a warrior on a mission, and I got my driver's license.

I soon started working and moving up the job ladder. I managed to juggle my new forty hour–plus job with household chores and caring for my one- and two-year-old babies after day care. I thanked God for my professional success and the steady income that I so desperately needed to gradually make ends meet. But confusion, emptiness, and sorrow were still my companions. I began to long for the freedom and flexibility of being with my daughters. It was the entrepreneurial itch.

The *security* of where I was and the *insecurity* of where I wanted to go were holding me back. We're taught to find believable, objective, and realistic goals rather than dreams that are too big and based on erratic illusion.

I once heard someone say, "'But you are so good at it' are perhaps the cruelest words ever spoken." I believe that's true. Skills alone don't guarantee fulfilling, sustainable success. Because you were born to be a conscious creator, you can only find fulfillment through doing work you are passionate about, work that brings you joy while creating true value for others. We must develop a conscious awareness of how false security may be hindering our sacred purpose.

I heard a voice within me say, *If God gives you a vision, He has given you permission to create it and will give you the provision for you to see it manifested.* I decided to believe that voice. After tuck-ins, nightly prayers, and good-night kisses, I started working on my business. My goal was to invest ten minutes each night and ten dollars a month. I took inspiration from Theodore Roosevelt's words: "Do what you can, with what you have, where you are."

Within a few months, I finally decided to take the leap from being a slave to a paycheck to actually profiting from my passion. What started out as a web design business has evolved over the years. I now serve as a mentor, trainer, and coach to moms all over the world who wish to turn their pain into prosperity, because every step of the journey is part of a beautiful eternal puzzle.

I'm in a state of constant gratitude and awe for my many blessings, knowing that my business model supports the lifestyle I desire: staying at home, enjoying the family togetherness I so deeply craved, homeschooling my daughters, having the freedom to offer them a life on our own terms, and supporting their own entrepreneurial journeys.

And after "acting as if" (or what I call "faithing it") to be a positive role model for my daughters, I was truly able to find joy in the journey, to enjoy entrepreneurial freedom again, to write stories again, to empower audiences with positive messages, and to help moms succeed with my teachings, guidance, and support.

I sought a supportive environment, mentors, and partners who challenged me to truly pursue my greatest purpose. And when I heard Janet speak about the Passion Test at a conference, I knew I was living proof of someone who was truly living her passion. Yet that little voice inside spoke to me again... and I had to listen. It said, *Our daily decisions determine our direction and our destination.*

I followed Janet to her Passion Test workshop, and in just a few minutes, my life was transformed. When she first suggested we include our ideal "love life" on our list of passions, I didn't see that happening. I wrote my list of ten answers, but there was unrest in my soul.

Janet's energy and the safe place she created in that small Chicago hotel room suddenly prompted me to make a decision based on a vision of love and not out of my fear. I hadn't admitted in a while how afraid I was of the frustration, brokenness, and despair I had experienced in my relationship.

I thought of the Jewish proverb, "What the daughter does, the mother did." Did I want to teach my daughters that...

- relationships are a waste of time?
- there are no honorable men left?
- I didn't believe in second chances?

So I scratched out an answer about career success and wrote my number three passion in its place. My top five passions turned out to be

1. Being deeply connected to God, self, and the people in my life;
2. Living a joyful, united, meaningful life with my family;
3. Experiencing a peaceful, loving, and mutually empowering relationship with my eternal partner;
4. Enjoying abundant time, energy, and resources to play, connect, and contribute generously; and
5. Equipping, empowering, and encouraging moms worldwide to increase their impact, income, and influence so that they can create a legacy of JOY, BALANCE, and SUCCESS on their own terms.

That last passion was a mouthful, but owning the third one brought me to tears. I realized I had an outrageously passionate life, but I really did desire a loving relationship based on commitment, affection, appreciation, support, freedom of expression, and mutual care. I wasn't living that passion, and I was sabotaging myself by operating from the relationship stories of my past and settling for a false sense of empowerment: *I can do it alone.*

Taking the Passion Test gave me the clarity I needed to discern exactly what the terrifying road ahead looked like. I was trembling when I wrote *falling in love, getting married,* and *having a baby* as markers, yet it took less than a year for all three of these to manifest—and in that order.

The Passion Test brought my life full circle. I realized that I didn't have to sacrifice one passion to live another. My passions are clues to my God-given purpose, and now that I am unquestionably clear on what they are, I can enjoy them all. And so can you.

In my mentoring practice, I take moms worldwide through the Passion Test as a foundation to deliberately creating a life by design. It is truly the first step toward defining what JOY, BALANCE, and SUCCESS look like... on your own terms.

When you're clear about your passion, you make a decision to be positive and generate the fuel to be powerful. Are you ready to reclaim your power?

Elayna Fernández, known worldwide as the Positive MOM, is an award-winning storyteller, a renowned digital strategist, and an avid student of pain. Elayna helps moms rewrite their story, heal their wounds, and create joy, balance, and success on their own terms – in all areas of life. Elayna encourages, empowers, and equips moms to increase their impact, income, and influence, without guilt, shame, or regrets.

Born and raised in a slum in the Dominican Republic, Elayna now lives in Fort Worth, Texas, with her loving husband and 3 homeschooled daughters. Elayna is often featured in global media and travels the world as a motivational keynote speaker and Success Principles trainer for moms.

Elayna has been awarded as Best Marketer, Mom Entrepreneur of the Year, Best Latina Lifestyle Blogger of both 2015 and 2016, and named one of the Top Latina Influencers in the USA. To learn more about Elayna, visit her highly acclaimed blog, thePositiveMOM.com.

Chapter 14
HAWAIIAN REBIRTH—WITH A SNAP OF THE FINGERS

Yves Nager

"*Love yourself, be good to yourself, others, the earth and the life of the earth, and remember – WELL BEING IS A FEELING!*
—**Howard Wills**

I heard a soft voice say, "You look so beautiful now, and the color of your eyes has changed."

When I opened my eyes, I found that I had woken up in paradise. I saw I was reborn into the most beautiful world. I felt like I was waking up in another dimension or reality. There was no difference or separation anymore between how I felt deep within and what I perceived in the outside world. I felt one with creation and the Creator. All the pain, all the struggles, all the suffering, and all my feelings of separation and inadequacy were completely gone. All my senses were crystal clear as never before, and tears of gratitude were flowing down my face.

I realized the very loving and caring voice belonged to the person who had guided me to this magical place less than two hours earlier. With the help of Paul, I had found myself again, inside an opening in the tropical forest above Honolulu, Hawaii.

With a gentle smile in his eyes, Paul said, "Watch this now," and he raised his right hand and snapped his fingers.

With amazement, I looked up to see the clouds making way for a patch of blue sky right above us. The clearing in the trees we were standing in was immediately filled with a huge bright column of light. Paul snapped his fingers again, and now we found ourselves in absolute silence. Just moments earlier, the whole space had been full of the melodic chatter of singing birds. I was absolutely present and experienced the power of the moment more profoundly than ever before. A few moments later, Paul snapped his fingers once more, and instantly, the birds started to sing again, the opening in the sky closed, and the clouds returned.

Paul said, "Yves, it is now your turn to try. You can do the same."

Although I was doubtful that I could create such a miracle, I put my trust in this magical new friend and snapped my fingers. I watched again in awe as the same column of light came down to fill the clearing and the birds stopped singing until I snapped my fingers again. I was blown away and felt like I was dreaming. This was the biggest miracle I had experienced in my whole life.

How is all of this possible? Who is Paul? Why is this happening today? And will this beautiful dream last forever? These were some of the questions running through my head, and I asked them of Paul while we were driving back to Honolulu.

Paul smiled at me again and said, "It is possible because of Aloha Ke Akua."

"Paul, I just got here two weeks ago, and I am not yet familiar with the Hawaiian language. Could you please explain to me what that means?"

"It means to recognize God as the Supreme Being, to acknowledge the divine spirit in all things, and to be grateful for its many blessings."

While Paul spoke these words, I felt as though the divine itself was speaking to me.

Paul continued. "We were brothers in another lifetime here in Hawaii. In that lifetime you helped me, and now I am here to help you."

"I was struggling for thirty-two years. Why didn't we meet earlier?"

"Because you chose to experience it today."

"I feel so wonderful now. Will it last forever?"

In the meantime, we had arrived near the ocean, and it was almost sunset.

"Yves, look out at the ocean and the waves. It will be just like the waves—sometimes high and sometimes low. Sometimes you will feel as wonderful as you do right now, and then you will find yourself feeling disconnected again. However, even when you feel low, always remember that you are like a drop of water, part of the ocean, and will be carried through the low and high tides of life."

Paul had to hurry to catch his flight back home to the Big Island, and our time together was running out.

"Paul, all I wish for is to do the same thing you just gifted me with. What do you recommend as my next step?"

"Learn and practice energy and healing work, and you will start to create and share the same experiences for others."

"When will I be ready?"

"Whenever you choose to be ready."

Paul smiled at me one last time, gave me a long, loving hug, and then drove away. I sat down by the ocean, gazing at the gorgeous sunset. I felt more clarity, peace, and inner calm than ever before, and I tried to recapture what I had just experienced. It was only four days ago when Wendy, my host in Manoa Valley, told me she had received a phone call with an important message for me. Paul told her he was having very vivid dreams and visions about someone staying at her place, and he needed to come to help this person immediately. The description of the person in his dreams fit me. Of course I said yes to his offer of help. And four days later, on this magical afternoon, Paul showed up at the door in a truck that even carried a massage table. How did he manage to bring that table? Regardless, it was where much of our work together took place.

During my sunset contemplation, I also wondered if I would see Paul again. Later, I tried my best many times to locate and contact him; however, I never saw him again. Now it was up to me to make this dream last forever, and to remember that I am a part of this ocean of love always surrounding me.

This fateful meeting with Paul in 2008 changed the course of my life, and started me on my mystical journey of healing and transformation. This remarkable experience gifted me with a rebirth, after a time of crisis and desperation reached a climax when a series of deaths occurred in my family in 2005. Within only seven months, I lost my father and two grandparents, and I almost lost my brother as well. After that, life was never the same again. I immersed myself in work by day and partying by night on the weekends in a futile attempt to free myself from the uncomfortable feelings of loss and pain. I lost direction and wasn't sure what, if anything, would bring back my sense of purpose or passion for life. While my personal relationships and career succumbed to more chaos and dissolution, I kept searching for meaning but was gripped by massive depression to the point of even considering ending my own life.

On Christmas Day, 2007, I started to pray desperately for help and guidance, something I had not done for years. Only ten weeks later, I found myself on the island of Oahu, Hawaii. Before I left my home in Switzerland, I had worked as a human resources manager and was responsible for more than 650 employees. On my last workday, my successor, Oliver, gave me two books. The first book I started to read as soon as I arrived on Oahu was *The Power of Now* by Eckhart Tolle, which I followed with *The Secret* by Rhonda Byrne.

Since my early childhood, I had a knack for making things happen with my focus, aka manifesting. When I look back, I realize I did it mostly unconsciously and without clear intention. Therefore, the results were mixed—both amazing and disastrous experiences, which were still blessings in disguise and gave me many lessons to learn. I never clearly understood why I would experience amazing miracles and bliss at times, and then plunge to the bottom of the emotional scale, desperate and wounded through some external circumstance that I thought I had no control over.

After many years of doing my best to become a conscious creator without consistent results, I realized why I still created outcomes I didn't intend after applying what I'd read in *The Secret* during my first visit to Hawaii in 2008. For example, I really wanted a girlfriend from Hawaii right after my meeting with Paul, and I attracted one. But we were both too tense and unclear about who we really wanted to become, let alone what we were looking for in a relationship. Therefore, my dreams of finding a soul mate and building a lasting relationship were dashed. After the temporary high and bliss of having just found a beautiful woman, I found myself hurt and depressed for a few weeks after our breakup. I was living in paradise but felt disconnected and started looking desperately for Paul so that he could help me again. I tried many things to get myself back on track, but no matter how hard I tried, nothing worked.

It took a pretty drastic decision for me to finally break through. I went skydiving, and after my second jump, with a lot of adrenaline in my body, I finally got more clarity for my remaining time in Hawaii. My intention was clear. After riding an emotional roller coaster, it was time to learn more about healing, as Paul suggested, and be crystal clear about what kind of relationship I wanted.

When I studied Presence Centered Awareness Therapy on Kaua'i in 2011, I realized how important it is to let go and relax in order to experience healing with ease and grace. I realized that, just like me, many people suffer because of their way of thinking about their past experiences, which already lost their true impact a long time ago. I learned that suffering originates from the unwillingness to let go of the stories we tell about our past experiences.

One of the best tools I learned for letting go of the stories of the past is Ho'oponopono. It is an ancient and very powerful tool for forgiveness and peacemaking originally used within families. Its roots are thousands of years old, and it is part of a Hawaiian healing system called Huna. The native priests and wisdom keepers of Hawaii, called "kahunas," say that thoughts are physical, alive, and have substance, even though they are invisible. Your thoughts are powerful and influence your feelings; they manifest as health or illness in your being. The remedy is to have simple, happy, positive, nonjudgmental thoughts and feelings.

After I finished my studies on Kaua'i, I went on a profound spiritual vision quest throughout Hawaii, as part of giving back to the Hawaiian lands and further activating my own healing power. During that journey, through divine synchronicity I met a Hawaiian kahuna in a remote valley on Molokai.

I asked him, "Pilipo, I always wanted to meet a wisdom keeper like you. Could you please tell me more about Hawaiian wisdom?"

He answered, "Yves, the most important thing is that just to know something and not to act accordingly is like not knowing anything at all. Wisdom always gets revealed *when you take action upon what you know to be true.* Ho'oponopono is a simple tool to help you take action in order to cleanse yourself of grief, fears, and destructive habits."

Here are the first four simple and practical steps Pilipo shared with me. You can apply them whenever you have a conflict, problem, or disharmony blocking you from moving forward toward living your passions.

1. Go within and meditate. *Pray* to receive insight, courage, power, intelligence, and calmness.
2. *Describe the problem* honestly and start searching for *your contribution* to it. It might be an opinion, a behavior, or a memory that you need to look at and heal.
3. *Forgive yourself and anyone else* involved in the problem completely, totally, and unconditionally by repeatedly speaking the four following statements: "I am sorry. Please forgive me. Thank you. I love you."
4. *Express gratitude.* Give thanks, trust, and let go. Shift to a relaxed space of "no tension."

Later, when I became a Passion Test facilitator, I learned that both Nature's Guidance System and The Work of Byron Katie provide the same results of finding peace with self and others as Ho'oponopono does.

I took Pilipo's words of wisdom to heart and started practicing this ancient ritual of forgiveness and gratitude. I cleared energy of heartache from a series of failed relationships and was getting ready to be my best self in the ideal relationship I envisioned. I also started to write down the qualities I wanted in my ideal partner. In October of the same year, through another series of divine synchronicities that, looking back, were fueled by Intention, Attention, and No Tension, I got together with my beloved Eunjung in Kaua'i. You can read the full story of how we were guided to each other on www.crazylovestories.com.

It was much later, the end of 2014, when the missing pieces finally fell into place. That was when Eunjung and I went to a Passion Test facilitator certification course in San Rafael, California, and learned the Passion Test formula: Intention, Attention, No Tension. Since my magical healing experience with Paul, I had been much more aware of how to consciously choose (intention) and how to focus (attention) on what I really wanted in my life. However, through the Passion Test facilitator course, I started to connect the dots between this principle of creating from a place of no tension with the principles of intention and attention.

Since Eunjung and I became facilitators for the Passion Test, Passion Test for Business, and Passion Test for Kids and Teens, we have had several opportunities to spend time with other Passion Test family members. In the Hawaiian language, a family is called "ohana," which is defined as "several plants with a common root." Each of us is not only part of our family of origin, but throughout life we also become a part of other families, such as work or school. Why do we Passion Test facilitators call ourselves a family? I think it's because we share common values—inspiring transformation through love and following the principles that lead to living a passionate life. Why do we need to be surrounded by people who hold dear the principles of living a passionate life and following your heart? If you're trying to live a life of passion by yourself, you may get easily discouraged or distracted in the face of internal challenges or naysayers around you.

After my first return from Hawaii to Switzerland in 2008, people who knew me from before told me I "better become normal again." However, after my profound transformational experience, I had no choice but to stay true to my heart's calling and deepen my journey of healing for others and for myself. When you are surrounded by others who follow the same principles of the heart and live a passionate life, you can support and encourage each other, and you won't feel alone. If you want to achieve your goals and ultimately fulfill your life's purpose, you must stick to your dreams and refocus on what you are most passionate about. I am grateful that I am part of and supported by our Passion Test family and friends. Our connection also creates a safe environment to express the uncomfortable emotions that I, like all of us, face when I reach for my deepest heart's desires. Let me leave you with six practical steps based on the six letters contained in the word "family":

F: Follow your heart and passions, share them with others, and have fun with it.

A: Every day find things you appreciate about yourself and others, and put them into affirmations.

M: Meditate daily, become aware of the miracles in your daily life, and start magnetizing them.

I: Have incredible intentions. Keep thinking and speaking about them, and write them down.

L: Love is the most powerful force in this universe. Love yourself, love others, and love life itself.

Y: Say Yes to life and your passions whenever you're presented with an opportunity, decision, or choice.

As I look out the window at the majestic Mount Wai'ale'ale (the summit is one of the rainiest spots on earth), the beautiful flowers in the trees, and the turquoise ocean off Kaua'i, I'm reminded of the abundance of life itself. I can hardly believe the incredible transformation I have gone through in the past ten years. Now I'm doing healing work with both people and animals, just as Paul predicted. I'm facilitating the Passion Test with individuals and companies around the world and have traveled to more than thirty countries with my beloved partner, teaching workshops and leading ceremonies at sacred sites. Together, we're making our unique, inspired contribution to creating heaven on earth.

I am excited about what is possible and how my life will look in another ten years, and what legacy I will leave behind when I cross over the rainbow bridge, as the Hawaiians say. What I know is that with the crystal clarity of my life's vision that I gained using the Passion Test, I'll be navigating my life with my passions as the compass, trusting my heart's ability to sail through the low and high tides of the ocean waves, stormy or calm, and ultimately enjoying the greatest adventure as a conscious creator. My last invitation to you is to ask yourself these same two questions: How will my life look in ten years, and what legacy would I like to leave behind?

Yves Nager is a gifted healer of both people and animals, Passion Test and Passion Test for Business facilitator, certified Dream Coach, Discover the Gift trainer, and Yoga Nidra and meditation teacher. He is passionate about supporting people in transcending limitations to gain new possibilities and transforming challenges into freedom. He understands the power of forgiveness and gratitude, and how focusing on your heart's desires and intention leads to creating miracles. Yves is dedicated to helping you discover your unique gifts

and live your life with even more passion, joy, and abundance. Yves is the author of the ebook, Find Your Life Purpose! 7 Steps and 12 Questions to Fulfill Your Destiny. *He lives on Kaua'i with his beloved, Eunjung. His website is www.yvesnager.com.*

Chapter 15

MANIFESTING MAGIC

Ratika Hansen

"Manifesting is a practice which contains a dose of magic and mysticism and a ton of being open to what might be."
— **Nancy Alder**

*W*ill that be all today?" she asked, as she scanned his one and only item.

"Yes, just the salmon, please. How've you been? How is the running going?"

"Good. In fact, my husband and I are training for the Shamrock Run next month—and our kids are joining us!"

"Are those your kids?" he asked, observing the photo buttons on her apron.

"Yup."

"Are they twins?" he asked, noticing how close they looked in age.

"They are," she said with a proud smile.

"You know, my wife and I want to have twins, but we need a surrogate."

"You know, I looked into being a surrogate last year."

"You did? Maybe you and my wife should talk," he suggested.

"Maybe we should," she agreed with another smile. And she gave him her phone number.

• • • • •

Twenty minutes later...

"What's for dinner, handsome?" I asked, as my husband walked through the door.

"Salmon... Oh, and I think I found our surrogate." He announced both in the same casual tone.

Intention, Attention, No Tension

And it happened... just like that. A month later, we began the process of bringing the miracle of life into our family with the generosity of a very special woman and her supportive family.

Now this is *not* the way I thought we were going to find our surrogate. A couple of months prior, my husband and I went to the fertility clinic to discuss our options and left with a packet that included a list of websites where we could begin looking for our surrogate. My methodical mind had a plan to create an interview sheet and envisioned meeting with ten, twenty, if not fifty women to find *her*. I mean, you don't just ask any random woman to carry your babies. In my mind, this was going to be a very detailed and lengthy process. And it was a process that I was not ready to begin yet, as we had just closed on a house and were a few short weeks from moving.

I decided to put this on the back burner. All the while, my husband and I talked about her, dreamed about her, and brainstormed about the qualities we would want her to have, the habits and mindset with which she would already be living her life, to ensure our babies were well taken care of from the very beginning.

Imagine my surprise when he strolled in with our salmon dinner and the news of his serendipitous discussion with the woman at the store. Fortunately, I had been living by my favorite principle from the Passion Test—*Stay open to how your passions are getting fulfilled*—for a few years and was open to finding our surrogate through my means—or anyone else's. Without skipping a beat, I smiled and replied, "Really? Tell me more." A few days later, I met with our soon-to-be surrogate and found her to be even more amazing than we had dreamed. It truly was the beginning of a very beautiful relationship.

This is, so far, the most remarkable example of Intention, Attention, No Tension playing out in my life. My husband and I had the clear *intention* of finding a surrogate—we wanted children, we knew that I couldn't carry them, and we wanted to use a surrogate. Then we put our positive *attention* on that intention. It wasn't a ton of attention, but it was all positive. We met with a fertility specialist to learn the process. We talked about our surrogate often, creating our relationship with her every day in our conversations. I began putting money aside each month for the journey we were about to begin, in an account I named "Babies." And after that, we sat back in *no tension*, open to accepting the actualization of our intention in any way it came to us.

Although I had a plan, I was not exclusively bound to it as the one and only way to find our surrogate—thank goodness! Had I held tightly to my plan, I may not have even heard what my husband said as he walked through the door that day, much less entertained the idea of meeting with her before I had begun my own process. Being clear, positive, and open led us to meet the woman who so graciously blessed us with the family we cherish today, beginning the process even before we moved into our new home.

Shifting My Perspective on Perfection

That new home was another wonderful example of Intention, Attention, No Tension. My husband and I had been talking (yes, we talk a lot!) about moving into a new home before starting our family. We talked about the kind of house we wanted, the features it would have, and the type of neighborhood we wanted to move to. That was about as far as we got when a friend of mine asked me how the house-hunting was going. "It just picked up," I replied as I went online, while still on the phone with her, to search for homes on the market. I found eight that I liked and printed out copies of their listings. When my husband came home from work that day, I showed him the listings and we narrowed the list down to four.

The next day, we drove to the first house—to find that it was only being shown to people who had realtors with them. I called ours but got her voicemail. So I left a message and my husband and I agreed that if she got the message and was able to help us, wonderful. If not, then there was a better house out there for us. We proceeded to check out the second house and, unimpressed, headed to the third when our realtor called us. She was on her way. We met her at the first house, walked through it, and fell in love. I remember saying, "This is where our babies will play," as I pointed to an open area upstairs. We left the house and drove straight to our realtor's office to write our offer—the fourth for the sellers to consider.

As we drove home that evening, we easily could have freaked out. Our walkthrough was very quick—did we overlook anything? We had only looked at one other house—were there better options out there? Our offer was a shot in the dark—did we offer too little? Or worse—too much?

Again, in the space of Intention, Attention, No Tension, we got clear about the kind of house we wanted, found one, and submitted an offer. And then we told ourselves that if the offer was accepted, this was the perfect house for us. And if not, there was another, better one waiting for us. We trusted deeply that by holding positive energy around our new home, we would attract the very best one for us. The next day, our offer was accepted and we bought the house that we brought our babies home to almost two years later.

The Power of Clarity

The first time I did the Passion Test, I was single, and one of my top five passions was about spending time with the man of my dreams. A year later, when I attended my Passion Test facilitator certification course, I was engaged to be married.

During the course, I went through the Passion Test process again, and much to my surprise—and concern—this time, "the man of my dreams" was nowhere on my list. My gut reaction was to do it over—surely, I had made a mistake. But one of the course assistants encouraged me to keep moving through the process and dive deeper into what I was feeling. I realized that whereas I saw dating as a fun and playful time, I saw marriage as a stern commitment that required constant focus and discipline—meaning some seriously hard work. This awareness gave me the opportunity to talk to married women about my naïve perceptions of marriage and what it really takes to make it successful. These conversations taught me that although marriage *is* hard work, it can also bring a connection like nothing I had ever experienced before. The sobering significance that I had put on making my marriage "work" was replaced with inspired excitement to make it thrive. Equipped with this new knowledge and positive perspective, I walked down the aisle a year later a beaming bride.

A few years later, however, the glow had faded. As I stared sadly at my top five passions, trying to figure out why I felt so empty and disconnected, I found my number one passion staring me in the face. It was about spending time with my husband. I had been living with my marriage as my number one focus, and in the process, I had lost myself. Once I recognized that I could ignite greatness in my marriage only to the extent that I had it in me, it was easy to see the importance of lighting my own fire first. Empowered with this newfound wisdom, I went through the Passion Test process again, and a new number one passion emerged about feeding my soul. This was the beginning of reconnecting with myself and coming alive again. It was also the beginning of a new chapter in my marriage and in my life.

Time and again, the Passion Test has enabled me to uncover misguided paths that I have unknowingly put myself on and chart new, more conscious courses focused on joy and fulfillment. I trust the power of the process to reveal thought-provoking questions that deepen my self-awareness and increase the clarity with which I lead my life. This investment of trust has paid dividends in keeping me on the path toward living a passionate life.

My Current Top Five Passions and Markers

I take the Passion Test every year, because life circumstances and perspectives can change that often. Even if the essence of each passion remains the same, it's always interesting to see how I choose to phrase them from year to year. True to form and process, this year again revealed to me new learnings and considerations.

Since my top five passions had been quite similar for the last couple of years, I was sure to remind myself to open my heart to any and all possibilities of an ideal life.

The biggest surprise this time was that the Man of My Dreams passion, now the Marriage/Husband passion, moved from number two to number three on my list—not because our relationship was less important, but because I was acutely aware of how vital it was for me to guide our sons consciously in these very formative years. I knew that it would take great attention and focus to consistently shift my mothering approach from reactive and impulsive to mindful and compassionate—especially when I am stressed or tired. Perhaps my biggest realization from this session was that the energy I do devote to my marriage needs to be positive energy. If

I dwell on any frustrations, real or, in most cases, fabricated in my mind, I upset and irritate myself, setting a tone for failure in every other relationship in my life.

Here are the results of my most recent Passion Test, including my top five passions and their markers:

1. I am fueling my Light and shining it brightly in the world.
   a. I am filling my tank with Reiki, acupuncture, yoga, dance, journaling, and prayer.
   b. I am strengthening my physical body regularly through exercise and movement.
   c. I am grounding myself in my culture, with Hindi movies, music, food, and traditions.
   d. I am creating and following a schedule that allows time for everything that is important to me. I am feeling peaceful and calm in my soul.
   e. People are mirroring my "glow" with smiles and kindness.
2. I am guiding our sons with love, giggles, and mindfulness.
   a. I am continuously learning new ways to be a mindful mama.
   b. I am role-modeling healthy personal interactions.
   c. Our boys are growing into independent, responsible, brave, kind gentlemen.
   d. Our boys are feeling loved and expressing love often.
3. I am connecting with my husband to co-create our best life.

   a. I am graciously and genuinely inspiring him, supporting him, and encouraging him to be his best.

   b. We are talking a lot about our visions for the future, speaking it into being.

   c. We are enjoying date nights and trying new activities together.

   d. We are smiling, laughing, hugging, kissing...

   e. We are inspiring others to have love and joy in their partnerships.

4. I am connecting with family and friends often, feeding my network and our sons' village.

   a. We are regularly talking, Skyping, and having playdates with people we love.

   b. I am feeling like I am a part of something bigger than myself, experiencing the safety, support, fun, and joy of a community.

   c. Our boys speak fondly and with a sense of belonging about the people in their village.

   d. I am contributing meaningfully to the world.

5. I am feeling peaceful, pleased, and confident with our financial path.

   a. I am earning a lucrative income by inspiring and guiding people to live passionate lives.

   b. I am knowing clearly where we stand financially, our next steps, and our long-term goals.

   c. I am feeling proud of what we have accomplished financially.

   d. I am making financial decisions with confidence.

The clarity and self-awareness that the Passion Test offers is the first step in creating a life of joy and fulfillment. It can awaken your mind to the truths in your heart, even dynamically as your life path curves from here to there, if you allow yourself the freedom to dream about your most ideal life. In honoring the process, I have manifested magic time and again in my life, and I wish the same for you. Here's to *your* passionate life!

Ratika Hansen is a wife, dedicated mommy to her twin boys, and marketing manager at a high-tech company. She is also a long-standing student of personal growth, devoting the last fifteen years to learning from a variety of masters. Her life purpose is to shine her Light in the world, in the form of acceptance, laughter, inspiration, and love. As a certified Passion Test facilitator and credentialed Make a Difference seminar leader, she has inspired thousands of people to live passionate lives and bring their Light to their relationships, their careers, and their communities. Visit www.Facebook.com/ ToYourPassionateLife and www.ToYourPassionateLife.com for gifts of inspiration to brighten your day.

Chapter 16

WHAT TO DO WHEN
YOUR PASSIONS CHANGE

Geoff Affleck

Looking at my life in 2006 you might think I had it pretty good. I had a wonderful wife, a fabulous home on idyllic Salt Spring Island, British Columbia, and a business that produced a $100k income and gave me the summers off.

My business was unique—a traveling ski and snowboard school with eight hundred students and one hundred instructors. Each weekend, we took busloads of kids from Toronto to local ski hills, where we provided all-day instruction and supervision. I had been a ski instructor for twenty-five years, and owning this business was a dream come true for me.

It was my passion.

But what do you do when your passion changes?

Uh-oh. Suddenly, my dream business had become a burden. The stress of being responsible for all those kids on the ski slopes, of being dependent on the weather gods for my livelihood, and of the logistical challenge of living four months of the year in Ontario and eight months in British Columbia began to suck the life out of me.

I was miserable and my marriage was showing signs of coming apart.

Constant credit card juggling in the off-season and our supersized mortgage compounded all this stress at work. So my wife, Lesley, and I found ourselves looking for answers at the local bookstore. Although Lesley was already a self-help junkie, I had always been too "smart" to need anyone else's advice.

In *Smart Couples Finish Rich*, David Bach gave us a wake-up call with his Latte Factor®—the simple idea that the difference between accumulating wealth and living paycheck to paycheck is to put aside a few dollars a day for your future rather than spending it on little purchases such as lattes, bottled water, fast food, magazines, and so on.

In *Rich Dad, Poor Dad*, Robert Kiyosaki showed us that the key to financial freedom was to own assets that produced business income and investment income, as opposed to employment income or self-employment income (like I was earning).

Aha! I was starting to understand what I needed to do. But how?

That's when Lesley read T. Harv Eker's number one bestseller *Secrets of the Millionaire Mind* and announced that we were going to attend his three-day Millionaire Mind Intensive event in

Vancouver. Mr. Eker had very cleverly included two free tickets to the event with the purchase of the book, and the $2,590 savings was irresistible to her.

She was super-excited. I was super-skeptical.

"Why do you think these tickets are free anyway?" my ego said to her. "They're probably going to try to sell us a bunch of stuff at the event, you know."

"Try to be open," she said.

So off we went, with my ego kicking and screaming.

My ego was right. They did try to sell us a bunch of stuff: $12 books, $20 CDs, and $25 "money jars" were the warm-up offers before they hit us with the $2,000 seminars. With each carefully scripted offer from the stage, more and more smoke blew out of my ears, exacerbated by Lesley running to the back of the room waving her credit card. My defenses were at an all-time high.

But something started to happen to me as I resigned myself to being there. I began to open up, even high-fiving my neighbors and saying, "You have a Millionaire Mind!!!" as instructed by the polished trainer who had sold his pizza franchises and was living in a motor home so that he could be "financially free."

What struck me was that financially free people really do think and act differently from the rest of us. The logic of this argument was enough to satisfy my ego. It just made sense: if I could change my thoughts, reprogram my neural pathways (brainwash myself?), and become a better version of myself, then I could have it all, too.

Using a triangle diagram, the trainer explained how there were three things that you had to have if you wanted to get out of the financial rut that 99 percent of the audience was in. The formula was RV+RK+RY. First, you needed to have the Right Vehicle (RV) for earning income—and clearly my little ski school business wasn't it. Next, you needed to develop the Right Knowledge (RK) and skills. Made sense. Finally, and most importantly, you had to become the Right You (RY). And it was painfully obvious that I had a long way to go on this corner of the triangle.

After sleeping on this epiphany, I came to the seminar early on the last day. I went to the registration table and told the somewhat shocked staff member there, "Sign me up for the full meal deal."

"But we haven't announced the 'seminar special' yet," he said.

"Well, I know there's going to be a program and a special deal, so let's do this now before I change my mind," I replied.

Eighteen thousand dollars later, I embarked on a journey that continues to affect my life to this day. Over the next three years, I was a zealous participant at a series of seminars and camps with catchy names like Guerilla Business School, Enlightened Warrior Camp, Life Directions, Wizard Camp, Mind of Steel—Heart of Gold, and Train the Trainer, all designed to develop my RV+RK+RY. I even became a volunteer staff member, just so that I could immerse myself in the programs over and over.

I realized that I didn't have to figure it out all on my own. The smart way and the fast way to success was to do what others had already done—to learn from their mistakes, knowledge, and wins in order to accelerate my own.

At this point, my ego was feeling pretty smart: "Good decision, Geoff."

As part of my package I had weekly calls with a life coach named Karen from L.A. After pouring out my life story and current woes to Karen and listening to her advice (actually, she mostly asked me questions rather than giving advice), I made the decision to sell my ski and snowboard business. I told Karen that I had paid $80k for the business in 2001, and that I was willing to sell it for $200k, since sales had doubled and profits had tripled over the past six years.

"Nonsense!" she said. "Geoff, your net worth is a direct reflection of your self-worth. You're not only undervaluing your business at that price, you're undervaluing yourself. Double your asking price!" she counseled.

"Okay, coach." I gulped.

Three months later, I had a signed contract for $380k—$180k more that I was willing to sell for initially. At that moment, I had recouped the investment in my "$18k full meal deal" ten times over! That's why today I'm such a proponent of having a mentor or coach—the payoff can be incredible.

Fast-forward two years. Mortgage downsized by two-thirds— check. Credit cards paid off—check. Cut back on the "latte factor"—check. Invested in some "Rich Dad–style" real estate deals turned bad—uh-oh! Purchased a rather sketchy business coaching franchise and hating every minute of it—oops!

Looks like I needed a little more RV+RK+RY.

I was feeling lost. What was my life purpose? Was I even passionate about anything anymore? (I now skied once a year and hadn't found anything else that floated my boat.)

"What I am going to be when I grow up?" seemed to be an everyday question. I felt dead inside.

Then, while I was looking for answers at a seminar, Janet and Chris Attwood gave the audience an introduction to the Passion Test.

"That's it!" I said to Lesley, who had been patiently by my side as I squandered our nest egg. "If I can figure out my top five passions using the Passion Test like Janet says, then I'll be able to find work that I love, because this business coaching franchise is definitely not it!"

Janet and Chris explained that your passions are clues to your life's purpose—they are like breadcrumbs that lead you home. Seeking answers, Lesley and I both signed up for a four-day course to become certified Passion Test facilitators.

After taking the Passion Test, I discovered that my top five passions were:

1. Being of service to a massive number of people online,
2. Spending quality time with my wife,
3. Being a great dad (my daughter was born a year later, after ten years of trying to have a child),
4. Enjoying financial abundance, and
5. Sailing in warm waters.

You've probably heard the expression, "We teach best what we most need to learn." So that's exactly what I did. I facilitated the Passion Test process for people every chance I got. Whether it was a private session over the phone, a home party of five, a workshop of twenty, or a business audience of a hundred, each time I taught the Passion Test, I became more and more clear on my next professional move—the one that was aligned with my newly discovered number one passion.

Although Passion Test seminars were invaluable experiences, I knew in my heart that it was time for me to stop playing small and expand from making a local impact to making a global one.

Chris and Janet had become my new mentors and had taught me more than just the principles of living a passionate life. One Friday, while on a coaching call with Chris, I proclaimed, "I want to play bigger!" I told him about my passion for online marketing (even though I had very little experience doing it) and asked if he and Janet had considered creating an online Passion Test home study course. He told me that they wanted to create one but hadn't found the time or people to do it yet.

Chris and Janet teach the principles of creating an Enlightened Alliance. The key principle is that a lasting win-win business alliance can only be created when the critical needs of both parties are satisfied. In this instance, Chris and Janet's critical need was time. They had wanted to develop an online Passion Test video course but didn't have the time to do it. My critical need was to have an opportunity to play much bigger in the online marketing world and make a good living doing it.

So I wrote a proposal for a joint venture to develop an online home study course based on the Passion Test process, and they accepted it.

In 2010, our online course Passionate Life Secrets was launched in an intense, sleep-deprived, two-week online campaign. Having spent months developing the course, I was now thrown headfirst into the online marketing world: creating product offers out of thin air, scripting videos, writing copy, building web pages, sending mass emails, and setting up shopping carts. Words like "opt-in page," "autoresponder," "click-through rate," "conversion rate," and "affiliate commissions" were now part of my daily vocabulary, and I loved it! Was passionate about it, in fact!

During that launch, we added more than seventy thousand people to our email list, thanks to Chris and Janet's ability to engage affiliate partners who agreed to send emails on our behalf. We also created a live event because we needed a valuable bonus to help increase our sales. That three-day event was called Discover Your Destiny, and I was fortunate to be invited to speak there, sharing the stage with Janet and Chris, and some of the people that had influenced me along my short journey in the personal development world: John Assaraf, Marci Shimoff, and Greg Habstritt.

Since then, Chris and Janet have become my close friends and mentors. As I've continued to follow my passions for marketing and personal growth, I've constantly been blown away by the new opportunities that have come up. For instance:

- I've completely given up my local business coaching practice and now create online marketing campaigns and book launches for transformational leader clients worldwide.
- In 2011, I presented on the same stage as my former mentor, T. Harv Eker.
- With Janet, Chris, and Marci Shimoff, I co-facilitate the Enlightened Bestseller Mastermind Experience, sharing my knowledge with aspiring self-help authors.
- I've become a bestselling author.

I tell you all this not to impress you but rather to impress *upon* you the three things that have made the difference for me and for others both personally and professionally. I believe that if you adopt them, you will enjoy more happiness and fulfillment, too. They are:

1. **RV+RK+RY.** If you want to have a breakthrough when it comes to your career, then you need to have the right business vehicle and the right knowledge and, most importantly, become the right you.

2. **Get a mentor.** Investing in advice and coaching from those who've traveled the road before you will, without a doubt, help you play a bigger game than you could ever have played on your own. In my experience, good mentors are expensive, but the investment of time and money has been worth it every time!

3. **Follow your passions.** As Steve Jobs advised when he took the podium at Stanford Stadium to give the commencement speech to Stanford's 2005 graduating class, *"You've got to find what you love... [T]he only way to do great work is to love what you do. If you haven't found it yet, keep looking. Don't settle."* And that's where The Passion Test can help especially if you aren't sure what you are passionate about.

Now, ten years after Lesley dragged me kicking and screaming to that Millionaire Mind seminar, I can honestly say that I love what I do each day and am blessed to work with a heart-centered virtual team of colleagues and clients. At the same time, my life is still a work in progress—and I suspect that it always will be. After all, that's what a lifetime is for.

Geoff Affleck creates bestseller campaigns, product launches, and marketing funnels for contemporary thought leaders and authors. With New York Times bestselling authors Janet Bray Attwood, Marci Shimoff, and Chris Attwood, he co-facilitates the Enlightened Bestseller Mastermind Experience for aspiring self-help authors. He is the #1 bestselling co-author of Enlightened Bestseller: 7 Keys to Creating a Successful Self-Help Book, Breakthrough! Inspirational Strategies for an Audaciously Authentic Life, *and* Ready, Set, Live! Empowering Strategies for an Enlightened Life.

Geoff has shared the stage with T. Harv Eker, John Assaraf, Lisa Sasevich, Greg Habstritt, and Debra Poneman. He is a certified Passion Test and Passion Test for Business facilitator, and has an MBA from the Schulich School of Business in Toronto. Born in Australia, he now lives on Vancouver Island, B.C., and enjoys yoga, sailing, carpentry, and being present with his wife, Lesley and daughter, Skyla. Connect with Geoff at geoffaffleck.com.

CPSIA information can be obtained
at www.ICGtesting.com
Printed in the USA
LVOW11s2349050617
537062LV00002B/487/P